"This is my kind of book: Eart
Michael writes brilliantly and t
calling us out of our holy hudc
new generation. In a world of

book is another timely call to courageous, compassionate and
creative mission. And if such a call can possibly involve surfing
and getting a tan, so much the better."

Pete Greig, 24-7 Prayer and author of *Red Moon Rising*

"From kick-off you're grabbed by the scruff of your t-shirt and
carried along on a mission-adventure that you just can't put
down."

Andy Frost, Share Jesus International

"*God on the Beach* is a great read. It's a down to earth story of one
person facing their fear and stepping out in faith during three
summers of mission in Newquay. God's presence permeates the
missions and the pages of the book in gentle but very real ways.
It is this sense of God's presence that transforms Michael from a
reluctant, nervous member of the mission team to someone who
is able to join in with what God is doing in people's lives in
Newquay in some ordinary and very extraordinary encounters."

Jonny Baker, National Youth Co-ordinator (UK), Church
Missionary Society

"*God on the Beach* is an exciting account of mission on the edge of
the church. Here we find ourselves witnessing the vivid spiritual and relational realities of working with young people
today."

Dr Pete Ward, Kings College, London

"Michael's amusing and descriptive writing style allows the
reader to get a real feel for the many things going through his

mind as he grapples with his doubts and fears and witnesses God working in some amazing ways. I recommend this honest and engaging book."

Phil Williams, National Director, Christian Surfers UK

"There are two mistakes you can make with this book. One is not to read it. The other is to read it before going to bed. If you don't read it you'll miss out on a riveting story of young men and women taking risks to tell others about Jesus Christ and of God always being one step ahead, preparing the way. If you read it before going to bed, don't expect to sleep – your spiritual adrenalin will have got your heart racing for the people God wants to reach with his love and mercy."

Chris Cocksworth, Principal of Ridley Hall, Cambridge

God on the Beach

MICHAEL VOLLAND

survivor

Front cover design by Mark Prentice
Typesetting by Alliance Phototypesetters, Pondicherry
www.alliance-interactive.com

ISBN 1 84291 228 3

Survivor is an imprint of
KINGSWAY COMMUNICATIONS LTD
Lottbridge Drove, Eastbourne, BN23 6NT, England.
Email: books@kingsway.co.uk

Printed in the U.S.A.

For my wife, Rachel

Thanks

My profound thanks go to Jane Grayshon for her hard work and encouragement. Thanks also to the following people, without whom there would not have been much to write about: Andy Frost, Jeremy and the Bunce girls, Maggie Simpson, Paul Chowdry, Pete and Suzie, Anji, Paul and Matt, Chris, Tim, Sophie, Ian Nicholson, Rachel, Hannah and, of course, my Heavenly Father.

PART 1

Paddling Out

I volunteered to take part in a Christian mission in Newquay for dubious reasons. Months before the mission began I picked up a flyer with an attention-grabbing photo of a surfer on it. The words on the flyer announced: *Dawn Patrol: Radical mission to surf, skate and club culture: Newquay, Cornwall. July 2001.*

I was excited. I suppose I must have given some consideration to the word "mission" but what really grabbed me was the prospect of spending a week in the summer beside the best surf break in the country. I applied and was accepted.

July soon arrived and as I crawled along the congested M5 towards Newquay, dressed in my board shorts and flip-flops, apprehension about what being part of a mission might actually involve began to creep into my surf-saturated head.

My fears were straightforward enough. The prospect of doing anything embarrassing and the idea of having to get too spiritual were the main contenders. I was wrestling with some bulky questions about my faith and felt like a fraud for even thinking about being part of a mission team.

I dealt with all of the anxieties nicely: I refused to think about them too much. I concentrated on getting to Newquay. As soon as I arrived I'd go for a surf. I'd worry about the rest later.

After a dawdling drive down from London (along with, it seemed to me, everyone *from* London), I eventually found myself in the queue to get into Newquay itself. It was unbelievably long. The sun grilled the line of cars. We were often at a standstill for so long that people left their cars and had a chat with whoever happened to be behind or in front. One group of lads made their way up and down the column offering cans of lager for sale. The town would be heaving that week. Whatever the Dawn Patrol organisers had planned, they had their work cut out.

Eventually, after the most extreme wait to get into a place, ever, I surprised myself by finding a parking space. I pushed a heap of change into an eager meter and leapt around for a minute, glad to be free of the car.

My long-neglected surfboard was strapped to the car's roof bars. I freed it, grabbed my wetsuit and headed in the direction of the beach. I was celebrating two things from the core of my being.

One: I was no longer trapped in a sticky car in a huge traffic jam. Two: I was beside the sea instead of in polluted west London. I was tempted to burst into a run by way of celebration. I had arrived and would be surfing very soon indeed. I loved surfing. This was a big day. The fact that I was in Newquay to join a mission team tried to capture my attention but I pushed the unwelcome thought successfully to the back of my mind. Getting in the sea with my surfboard became my only goal.

The walk to the beach wasn't a long one. Newquay is not a particularly big place. The narrow pavements were congested and I had to watch out not to clip anyone with the nose or fins of my board. A steady stream of people passed me in both directions. There was a buzz in the air – a contagious aroma of expectation. I passed pubs and bars. They were already busy. Garish electronic jangling blared from games arcades. There were surf shops in abundance. Hostels and B&Bs displayed "Full" signs below "Surfer-friendly" banners.

At that moment I couldn't see how a Christian mission could be taken seriously or have any kind of meaningful impact in the town. It looked to me like everyone was perfectly happy and having a great time. Wasn't it a little arrogant for a bunch of Christians to assume they had something to say that all these people needed to hear? I felt confused and uncertain and wondered what I had been thinking when I volunteered for the mission. Was it too late to change my mind?

Soon I had cleared the town centre and, for a few moments, I was able to pick up my pace a little. It didn't last long. At a bend in the road I was slowed down by a bottleneck. The road was narrow, forcing pedestrians single file beside a line of cars. I shuffled along, minding my board and impatiently checking out the vehicles beside me. They were all either boy racer cars or customised VW camper vans. Topless lads were crammed into the cars listening to happy-hardcore in their Oakley shades. The roofs of the campers were stacked high with surfboards. A moment later I was through the jam. Relieved, I pushed on, turned a final corner and at last I could see it: There was the sea!

The instant I set my eyes on the water stretching away into the hazy distance where its gentle curve cut the clear sky from left to right, I felt I was greeting an old friend. Clean lines of swell were rolling in – perfect surfing conditions! I would soon be washing London and the long, hot drive out of my system. I was so eager to be surfing that it couldn't be soon enough. I sped up.

I passed, along with scores of others, beneath a

large banner. It was stretched over a high scaffolding arch and announced: *The RipCurl Boardmasters Competition.* This was a stage on the surfing world-tour and pros from all over the globe would be competing. There would be big prize money on offer. The action would be well worth watching.

The road, which was covered with a light dusting of sand, began to curl down towards the beach. Warm, salty air filled my nostrils. I imagined the feeling of taking off on my first wave. It would only be a matter of minutes before this became a reality. My heart beat faster.

Music, laughter, excited chatter, the crash of the waves and the squawking of scavenging seagulls grew louder and were joined by a loud, friendly mantra from a smiling girl offering free shots of Liptons iced tea from a dispenser strapped to her back.

I wove hastily through the milling bodies at the bottom of the road that rolled everyone down onto the edge of the crowded beach. Around me people were thrusting hands out at the smiling iced-tea girl. She was dispensing free tea as quickly as the small paper cups were tossed, empty, onto the floor to join a hundred others being crushed beneath the stampede of dusty flip-flops.

I pressed past lads with surfboards. Groups of

teenage girls were shrieking at each other. A pair of irritable parents was trying to shove a hulking big-wheeled baby-buggy through the sand.

I could smell Chinese food. Chicken and noodles were being fried in industrial-sized woks. Guys in board-shorts were stuffing noodles into their mouths from Styrofoam cartons at high speed. The smell of the food mingled with the familiar waft of sun-cream, the stink from an overflowing rubbish bin buzzing with wasps and a puff of grass being smoked by someone close by. I took in this detail in an instant and in passing. I didn't have space in my mind to think about food, however good it smelled. There were waves waiting to be ridden.

~

Set on rocks above the sand was a tiny, crumbling changing facility. I quickly found a vacant cubicle and contorted myself into my wetsuit. The suit was a titanium-lined winter steamer. This was August. I was boiling hot. Sweating profusely, I rolled my discarded clothes into a ball around my flip-flops. Clutching my surfboard, I evacuated the changing rooms and hurried in the direction of the sea. The clothes-ball got dumped on the sand beside a lifeguard station. I hoped it would still be there when I returned.

As I picked my way across the crowded beach my eyes scanned the sea. I momentarily fixed my eyes on a surfer. He had just taken off on a head-high wave. The ride only lasted seconds but it was confident – full of big, powerful turns. I was half-way to the water now. I dipped the nose of my board to avoid knocking into a guy who was putting litter into a black sack. Moving closer to the sea I observed the rafts of beginners floundering in the white water close to the shore. They were clutching clumsy foam hire-boards. The edge of the ocean was stuffed with their tumbling bodies. As I made a quick mental search for the best place to paddle out, a girl in a bright yellow t-shirt walked in front of me. A blue graphic stamped on the back of her t-shirt snatched my gaze. It showed a barrelling wave and the words: *Getting the gospel on the beach*. I gave the girl a second look, realising immediately that she must be a volunteer for the mission. Hadn't I come to Newquay to join her? She had a black sack in her hands and was now stooping to pick up an empty can. I refused to stop. Right then the mission was not at the top of my "to do" list. It was the reason for my being there but at that moment I had a different focus. The ocean was calling. I had to surf. And I had to cool off. The temperature inside my wetsuit was rising rapidly. I needed to be in the water.

~

I reached the edge of the ocean and bent down to fasten the leash of my surfboard around my ankle. The water lapped around my feet. Before plunging in and making for the line-up I turned and scanned the crowded sand. I picked out a dozen young men and women in matching yellow t-shirts. Each was clutching a black sack and was litter-picking hard. My conscience prickled uncomfortably.

I turned towards the waves and waded in. In spite of having been so desperate to go surfing, as I paddled out, the image of the litter-picking mission team nagged at me. I wanted to concentrate on having fun. And I definitely didn't want to be clutching a bin-liner instead of my surfboard. I tried hard to push thoughts of the mission out of the way until after I'd had a decent session in the waves. It wasn't easy. Something inside me couldn't let it go.

Two hours passed and I started to get hungry. The waves had been great but it was time to paddle in and find food. I stashed my board and wetsuit behind a burger van and bought some chips that I ate while taking in the scene on Fistral beach again. I was standing on a concrete plateau.

In front of me wide, sand-cached steps descended and quickly disappeared completely into the sand. The plateau, like the slope leading down to it, was thronged with people coming and going. Here, beyond the market stalls that had sprung up to complement the surf contest, a few shacks were selling beach-type stuff. Surfers were queuing for the open-air showers. Student lads were checking out girls. Girls were laughing at boys. A man with dreadlocks was selling hash-pipes of various shapes and sizes.

The beach was carpeted with baking bodies. They extended out from the base of the steps (those that arrived earliest and couldn't be bothered to go any further), down towards the sea and then away to my left, towards the other end of the beach, a mile or so in the distance.

Every inch of sand was occupied – if not with a person, then with discarded clothing, stereos, bottles of beer, cans of coke, footballs, packets of cigarettes and damp wetsuits. Dance music rolled across the acres of bodies. The music cascaded from speakers piled around an enormous video screen that beamed out lurid adverts for mobile phones and make-up. I pulled my eyes away before it hypnotised me.

As I looked back across the beach I realised that

young people dominated the scene. Some lay alone, others in couples, most in large groups. If the teenagers and young adults had at that moment, melted into one living being, and all those over twenty-five had done likewise, the young people would have made for one gigantic goliath against a very pitiful, wrinkly David. There would be no contest. Young people ruled on Fistral beach.

Onto this sweaty, chaotic carnival, the hot sun beat down from a cloudless sky. The atmosphere throbbed with hormone-fuelled excitement and the air was thick with expectancy. What antics would erupt in the town's bars and clubs once the sun had set and the beach was temporarily abandoned?

I spotted two more guys in yellow t-shirts. They were carting their rubbish sacks towards a large green army tent that was pitched on the sand. The tent appeared to be some kind of a base. Other young men and women, also wearing yellow t-shirts, were milling around at the entrance. The litter picking seemed to be finishing. It was a shock for me to discover that a week of mission in Newquay would involve trawling around the sand with a rubbish sack. It seemed too much like hard work and way too humiliating.

~

Until that point I had been able to push the "mission" part of being on a mission out of my mind almost completely in favour of surfing and generally chilling out. My attempt to ignore the fact that joining the mission would require hard work and commitment was rapidly becoming less of an option.

I shifted in my flip-flops and fiddled with the car key in my pocket. I needed to make a decision: Could I join this mission team or did I knock the idea on the head and spend a week surfing? The easiest thing would have been to walk away. Something, however, kept me from making that decision and I continued to stare at the mission team milling around on the sand.

If I was going to join the team, I would not only need to get used to the idea of doing some work, but I'd also have to make a start on resolving the anxieties I'd pushed to the back of my mind on the journey down.

I had had months to prepare for this mission but instead I'd only let myself fantasise about surfing. Now I was faced with the reality: a week of public Christian activity that would probably involve deliberately starting conversations with strangers about Jesus. The idea was almost unthinkable.

Somewhere inside me, however, a tiny part of me wanted to rise to the challenge. And it really was a tiny part. The potential for rejection and embarrassment almost paralysed me with worry. On top of that, doubts and questions buzzed around the inside of my head like flies.

I had no trouble with the *idea* of Christian mission and evangelism. The idea was great because ideas could be pushed around and made to feel comfortable. It was the *reality* of mission and evangelism that bothered me.

The word "mission", felt familiar but the prospect of acting on it felt strange and alien. It was as if I'd have to pretend to be someone else to allow myself to *do* anything about what I claimed to believe. It didn't help that the church I had been sporadically attending in the months leading up to that moment was on the sleepier side of sleepy. I wasn't exactly what anyone would call "fired up".

I decided to pray. Given the circumstances I would need a clear, rapid response by way of guidance. I had just about enough faith to believe that God was aware of my predicament and could send some guidance my way. My prayer was short and (I thought) to the point. It went along the lines of: "Lord, if you want me to be part of this mission you'll need to show me. If you don't then I'll assume it's better that I go surfing. . . Amen."

I looked up at the waves rolling in, decorated here and there with standing surfers. A solid week of surfing was tempting. Mostly because deciding to do that would have been simple and easy. That plan, however, would require a room in a B&B and all the ones I'd seen had been full. . . Not so easy after all.

As I stood wrestling with guilt about missing the litter pick, doubt about the depth of my faith, worry about the possibility of talking to strangers, and general frustration about the whole situation, I spotted a familiar face among the crowds. It was a friend of mine – a guy called Matt. Matt was walking across the sand towards the steps where I was standing. He was wearing a yellow t-shirt. So Matt was on the mission! I'd heard months before that he was considering it but I was shocked to actually see him there.

He hadn't seen me but if I stayed where I was he soon would. I had approximately twenty seconds to make a decision. Did I stay or go? My eyes were fixed on him. I weighed the situation up. Matt was a DJ, a good DJ at that – and a top bloke. If he was on the mission team then perhaps the mission could be OK.

Matt was at the bottom of the steps. I had less than three seconds to turn around if I wanted to duck out.

He was two steps from the top.

I stepped in front of him, partly blocking his path.

"Matt!" I gripped his arm.

"Michael!" His face lit up. "Good to see you mate. How's it going?"

That was it. Decision made. There was no backing out now – not without an explanation anyhow. I would be joining the mission team. Feeling relieved that I'd made a decision at last, I aimed a mini thank you at God for the guidance that had arrived in the shape of Matt.

I was sure Matt would be struggling with many of the same things as me. It looked like God had put me in good company for the week. I wondered how long it would take me to discover why I was there.

Bedrooms and Big Hair

A gentle whiff of sweat and dirty socks hung in the warm air. I was standing in the doorway of a room that resembled a badly burgled house. Clothes and luggage were strewn everywhere and bedding dangled from the stacks of chairs that lined one wall. This was the lad's room – my accommodation for the week. There was a solitary toilet but no shower which, given the already-ripe odour, made me think that we wouldn't be spending too much time in bed (or anywhere even close for that matter).

The room was in the Newquay Christian Centre (aka: the NCC). It was a large, newly refurbished building, tucked away on a narrow road just above the high street.

The others had dumped their stuff (literally) earlier in the day. I cleared some floor space, stretched out my air mattress and sleeping bag and leant my surfboard in a corner on top of a pile of rucksacks. I looked at my tidy patch and grinned. It was an ordered island in a sea of luggage chaos. It wouldn't be difficult for anyone else to spot the well-trained, married man. Would my orderliness last the week? I doubted it. I took a deep breath and exhaled slowly, wondering what I had let myself in for.

Early in the evening my seven roommates appeared and we began to get to know each other before piling over to the dining hall for food. I had brought a set of decks with me and now discovered that along with myself and Matt there was another DJ on the team: Paul, aka Indian-Rubber-Man.

Paul was a quietly spoken hip-hop enthusiast who had arrived in Newquay accompanied by his lovingly packaged top-end mixer, which he claimed he would never play without. Matt and I nodded heavily as we admired the mixer's simple elegance. You could almost blow the cross fader from one side to the other. If Paul was good enough to use it anywhere close to the way it was designed to be used, watching him bring his tunes to life would be an unmissable experience.

The dining hall was at the other end of the building and would be doubling up as the girls' living space. Thankfully it smelled a whole lot more inviting than the lads' living space – for the time being at any rate. Girls, as everyone knows, can be even smellier than boys when it comes to communal living. Time would tell. . .

A few trestle tables had been laid up with plates and cups of squash. Two of the girls had made a chilli. An enormous hot pan appeared. People dived at it and helped themselves.

As I stuffed the food hungrily into my mouth, a girl named Kate mentioned that there would be a cooking rota for the week. I must have looked slightly shocked because she shot me a wide smile and explained that different people would be responsible for buying and cooking the evening meal each day. I racked my brains for ready recipes and drew a blank. My evening looked like being a fun one. . . salad and bread. Great! I was going to be popular. . .

We chatted about the first day of the mission as the food disappeared. Everyone had found the litter picking hard work, and not just physically (everyone except me, of course). Quite a few had struggled with feeling self-conscious. I was relieved to hear that. At the beach I had assumed they were all one type of Christian: super keen and certain. My own reservations had made me feel guilty, as if I was some kind of woolly Christian lightweight. I realised that perhaps I'd been being a bit hard on myself.

We talked about the other teams. Altogether, more than seventy young people between the ages of sixteen and thirty had volunteered for the Dawn Patrol mission. Everyone had been sorted into a team and been given a base in church and school halls across the town.

The teams were designed to cover the various aspects of summer life in Newquay. The street team would be doing questionnaires, dance and theatre in the town centre. The surf team would be manning the Christian Surfer's UK tent at Fistral beach. The arts team would be producing work for an exhibition and running an evening drop-in café. My team, the beach team, would apparently be working on Towan beach for the remainder of the week but no one around the dinner table was sure what exactly we would be doing.

We laughed and joked as the dinner debris was cleared away. I felt relieved that my teammates seemed to be approaching the mission with a sense of humour. It was beginning to feel like it could be fun as well as a challenge. I was still apprehensive about what being part of the mission might require of me and whether my relationship with God was even in the right place to see me through the week's challenges but at least it looked like I would be laughing as well as worrying.

Late that night, after some exploring in town and more getting to know each other, the members of the beach team piled back into the hall and crashed out all over the girls' sleeping bags to spend some time with Jem, our team leader.

Jem had big hair and a constant enthusiasm for everything. He'd arrived in Newquay with his wife and five daughters to plant a church a year before and had agreed to be part of Dawn Patrol on top of an already full (and noisy) life.

We chatted until the early hours of the next morning, pausing frequently for toast and cups of tea. There was plenty of laughing as Jem got us all talking about where we'd come from and what we did. Most people were students but a nurse, a youthworker, a computer technician and a semi-professional footballer had also volunteered.

As the night rolled on, Jem's conspicuous faith in God became obvious but what really interested me was that he wasn't in the least bit religious or up tight with it. Jem appeared to be a genuinely easygoing guy *and* a Christian. In my experience this combination was unusual. If he could keep it up and if I was able to witness a normal, cringe-free, out-of-the-closet Christian up close, it would be a potentially life-changing experience for me.

As people began to open up about their apprehensions, Jem told us about the first mission he'd been on.

Aged eighteen he had agreed to go on a mission thinking that because it was months away, he'd have plenty of time to make an excuse and get out of it. The months soon rolled by however, and before he knew it, he was in his battered Citroen 2CV driving to the mission, racking his brains about why on earth he'd agreed to do it and kicking himself for not coming up with a decent excuse.

As it turned out, the mission had been one of the most amazing weeks of his life. God did all kinds of crazy stuff and since then, he told us, he'd been on stacks of missions! He couldn't get enough of them apparently. . .

I had to admit that his was not an attitude that I'd come across before (although I could identify completely with part one of his story). To be honest, I didn't really want Jem's mission-keen-ness to rub off on me. After all, where would it stop? I wasn't certain that I wanted to be on the mission at all let alone feeling like I was at the start of a lifetime of them!

Listening to Jem's "my-first-mission" story worried me because he'd made it sound as if talking to strangers about Jesus was no big deal at all, and I had gone through school and university and into my first job absolutely certain that it was, surely, a very big deal indeed.

I had kept my faith in God a secret, almost convinced that to announce it would be verging on social suicide. I hadn't wanted to risk making my friends uncomfortable by being known as "the Christian" so I had opted for closet-Christianity.

My housemates at university knew that I sneaked off to church most Sundays but they probably put it down to eccentricity because I never really spoke about it and, as far as they could see, it didn't make all that much difference to the way I lived my life. This meant that although most of the time I didn't feel that I was being entirely myself, at least I wasn't freaking my friends out.

However, watching the mission team on the beach earlier that afternoon, thinking hard all day and then listening to Jem lifted a corner on the comfortable arrangement I had with myself. It was a fact that I *was* a Christian, so volunteering for a mission team meant not only admitting it but also doing something about it. Ideas like that scared me.

The conversation in the hall drew to a sleepy close. Everyone was knackered and we had a busy day ahead of us. As I crawled into my sleeping bag and lay in the dark listening to the other lads laughing and chucking stuff at each other, I sensed that some uncomfortable but perhaps overdue changes were waiting for me in the week ahead.

My mind flicked through my friends back in London and I imagined introducing them to someone like Jem in the pub. I was surprised to find I wasn't embarrassed by the idea of such a scene. The two separate worlds I inhabited – Christian world and real world – had a slim chance of meeting, possibly even merging, and remaining disaster-free.

I snorted inwardly at my day's odd events, offered a loud "goodnight" to the room, pushed in a pair of foam earplugs and fell into a busy, dream-filled sleep.

A Roaring Lion

Early the following morning, before breakfast, I was in my wetsuit on the empty, tide-washed sand of Fistral beach clutching my surfboard. I looked at the sky streaked with wispy vapour trails and breathed in the fresh, salty air. It was great to be away from the claustrophobic chaos of London.

There was a good swell rolling in and twenty or so guys were sitting in the water. I paddled out to join them and, as the sun rose higher and began to warm the air, I enjoyed an hour of decent surfing. Much too soon it was time to head in and back to the NCC. I would have to be quick if I wanted to grab some breakfast before all the teams gathered for a morning worship and teaching session.

I made it back with just enough time to wolf down a bowl of cereal. Dawn Patrollers were already filing into the NCC's main auditorium as I hurriedly pulled on some clothes and stashed my surfboard.

I sneaked into the busy auditorium as the worship was beginning and found my way to the back row. There, sitting alone, I felt I was a safe distance from anything too spiritual: if that was to happen it would surely take place further forward. I was partly joining in – I was after all, *present* – but I also comforted myself by being more like an observer. I would be able to filter out anything awkward or weird.

In front of me the auditorium was full of young people, many of whom sang enthusiastically. Some raised their arms and a couple of the more excited ones danced in the aisle. The band got into full swing, particularly the drummer whose facial expression convinced me that he could see things the rest of us couldn't. Plenty of people seemed to be passionate and certain. A few looked less certain. I was one of the latter.

The songs were familiar to me. I had sung them a hundred times at various churches and events over the years. I sang along with everyone else but inside I was wrestling with confused, self-conscious doubt rather than bursting with enthusiastic excitement. I began to worry that someone might come over and offer to pray for me: the spiritual retard. I was already praying though. In my head, as the music thumped on, I was trying to pull the wispy strands of my confused thoughts together and point them towards God for his attention.

"Help!" I prayed. "Lord, help me to make sense of being here. . . Why *am* I here? Where are *you*?"

God didn't give any sort of immediate answer that I could discern.

I sat down and put my head in my hands. That way at least I would appear spiritual if anyone looked at me. I hoped the session would soon be over so I could go and sit somewhere alone and think things through quietly.

The worship continued for almost half an hour. I just didn't seem to be able to make myself feel part of what was going on. As the band wound down and people around the auditorium began to sit, Andy Frost, the enthusiastic young guy whose vision Dawn Patrol had been, took to the stage to welcome us.

He spoke animatedly for a few minutes about the town and what we were here to achieve as young missionaries. He clearly believed that God wanted to do something awesome in Newquay that week and was going to use the mission teams in a big way.

Part of me was enthused by his words. I wanted to believe him. I wanted to be certain that God had brought us all together to do something special. But in order to be *really* sure I wanted to hear that from God himself, not from Andy, however excited he was.

Another part of me felt cynical. From the back of the auditorium, I was able to survey the gathered team members smiling at Andy's words and getting psyched-up for socking the gospel to Newquay. What, I wondered, if it was all just hype? What if everyone was only up for being part of an in-yer-face mission because they were surrounded by other people who were telling them that was how God wanted things done?

I was confused. I felt guilty for being cynical and naïve for wanting the mission to be worthwhile and successful. I put my head back in my hands.

At that point Andy announced that we were to spend some time praying. "Fine," I thought. Praying would be good – nothing would be demanded from me and perhaps, if I could concentrate hard enough, God would even give me some kind of assurance about what I was doing there.

I prepared myself to pray by not lifting my head from its place in my hands. Then Andy went and ruined everything.

We would, he announced, be praying in pairs and could we all find a partner as quickly as possible? My heart sank. I didn't want to pray with anyone else. What could I say for starters? "Lord, I don't know why I'm here. Amen." That would be a massive encouragement for whoever got saddled with me.

I looked up, hoping that everyone would have already found a partner, leaving me to pray alone. People were shifting seats to move closer to others. One or two glanced up at me, sitting at the back. I tried to return a look that said: "Don't worry about me. I don't need a partner. I'll be praying for all of you from back here. Alone. I'm very spiritual you know. . ."

Things seemed to be going well. No one was heading in my direction. But to my horror the threat didn't come from in front of me as I had expected. A sneaky prayer-partner came from behind. I'd thought I was safe from that direction! What was the point of sitting at the back if you could still be dragged into participation from your blind spot?

A woman in her mid-thirties wearing baggy

combat trousers and a confident grin came from what seemed like nowhere and slid along the row of seats until she was next to me.

"Hi!" she offered.

I smiled and returned the greeting innocently, as if I was completely unaware that I was sitting so far removed from everyone else and was without a partner.

We chatted for a moment and exchanged names. Hers was Karen. Karen then told me that she worked in the NCC. So! That was how she had managed to sneak up on me so craftily! She knew about a network of secret tunnels that could be used to pounce on unsuspecting doubters who sat at the back during services! Or, more likely, she had just happened to walk in from the office and decided to sit next to the closest person, which happened to be me.

Either way, I had a prayer partner and I would have to pray with her.

I decided to pray first to get my part over and done with quickly. I closed my eyes and rambled through something about the mission, trying to make it sound as spiritual as possible with all the right prayer-jargon. I Amen'd feeling quite pleased with myself.

It was then Karen's turn. She was silent. The

loud hubbub of other people's prayers filled the room. The pause continued long enough for me to look up and check that she was still there. She was. Her hands were resting on her lap, her head was bowed and her eyes were closed. I took a quick look around the room to assess where other people had got to and then quickly closed my eyes again as Karen began:

"Heavenly Father, you know this young man and you have a purpose for him."

This sounded like it could get a bit personal – a bit too close for comfort perhaps. . .

She continued:

"You know why he's sitting at the back here like a frightened mouse."

I tensed up. A frightened mouse! My fists clenched. *Me*? This was definitely too close for comfort and it was verging on offensive. How presumptuous of her to assume I had chosen to sit at the back because I was afraid. It was true of course, but she couldn't know that. . .

She pressed calmly on:

"Lord God, I pray that you would make this man like a roaring lion, not hanging round at the edges but getting stuck in where the action is. I ask this in Jesus' name. Amen."

I kept my eyes closed and my head bowed. Her

prayer had almost knocked me off my chair. I needed to gather myself. I had never come across anyone who was prepared to take that kind of risk and be so bold when they were praying with a complete stranger. I was embarrassed that she had spotted my fearfulness. Had it been that obvious?

I was silent. Then I knew I had a choice.

As I saw things, Karen's prayer was a large, well-filled sandwich: I could either pull it towards me and take a huge bite, or I could push it away.

It took me seconds to make up my mind. I grabbed at the prayer and made it mine.

"Amen!" I whispered. And in my heart I called out to God: "Please make it this way Lord. . . *Please.*"

Another decision quickly followed: I allowed myself to believe that God had brought *everyone* in the room, including me, to Newquay for a reason. This was a leap of faith and faith-leaps are a risky business. It was a case of reminding myself that God is way bigger than I often considered him to be and that, contrary to what I often imagined, God is active all the time and everywhere.

As I thanked Karen for her prayer, I began to consider more seriously what my part in Dawn Patrol would be. She smiled and touched my arm reassuringly before disappearing out of the auditorium as elusively as she had arrived a few moments before. I was left wondering about the timing of her arrival and the succinctness of the prayer. I also imagined that I had just had a tiny glimpse of God's sense of humour.

God on the Beach

Fifteen minutes after the prayers ended the beach team was standing in a yellow huddle on the sand of Towan beach. We clutched volleyball posts and nets, balls and several boxes of flyers.

Jem's plan was for one half of the team to find a place to set up the net and set a game of volleyball going while the other half wandered the beach asking people if they wanted to join in.

As we began to pick our way across the crowded sand I noticed that Matt had a surprising degree of enthusiasm as he looked out for somewhere to put up the net. He didn't seem to be all that bothered about the prospect of asking people to join in with the volleyball.

"How come you're so excited?" I asked. "Aren't you a bit nervous?"

Matt threw the ball he had been holding in the air and exhaled the word: "Nope!" diving forward to catch it. He missed and the ball bounced next to a group of bikini-clad girls who were chatting on mobile phones.

Matt may not have been nervous but I was. I wanted to scoop up some of his apparent confidence in the same way that he had just scooped the ball up from the sand.

"People like volleyball," he added.

I supposed he had a point. Volleyball was definitely a great game. Karen's prayer rolled through my mind. Perhaps I'd be able to shake off my worries once we got started.

A large part of my uncertainty stemmed from the fact that we weren't bringing a volleyball net to the beach because we just *had* to meet new people or provide something fun for them to do. We had an ulterior motive. We didn't only want people to play, we wanted them to talk. Or rather *we* wanted to talk about Jesus and we wanted them to listen. There were strings attached to our volleyball net. Strings that people might spot if they read the words on our t-shirts before they agreed to join in. What did Matt think about the strings?

He shrugged and threw the ball high into the air again.

"It's just volleyball," he said. "If people don't want to talk, they don't have to."

We had crossed a lot of beach by this point. Trying to find a decent sized empty spot to put up the volleyball net among so many people was taking longer than we'd thought. I was beginning to get used to the slightly confused stares we were drawing as the fifteen of us rambled along, dressed in identical yellow t-shirts. We must have looked like a group of foreign exchange students who didn't want to lose each other.

I was clutching a box of flyers. They advertised an event that Dawn Patrol would be hosting in a nightclub later in the week. From what I had been able to gather, the night looked like having an eclectic mix of music, a breakdance competition, a few testimonies and a prayer room for punters to hand in prayer requests. Having never been to anything remotely similar, I was intrigued to find out how the God/clubbing fusion would work out.

I was to hand out the flyers that afternoon but I wasn't sure that I'd know exactly what to say if someone asked me what the event would be like. Unlike most of the other clubs in Newquay, ours was unlikely to be full of people getting wasted on tequila and pulling their trousers down and I didn't want to mislead anyone. On the other hand I didn't want to be apologising as I handed people flyers. I decided not to think about what I'd say until I was actually saying it. I'd be interested to hear what I came out with.

Eventually we found a spot large enough to stretch out the volleyball net and mark off a rough court. Jem was focused. Before the court was finished, he was organising team members into pairs and encouraging them off to various parts of the beach armed with flyers and smiles.

Jem's plan was to get a league going. The plan also involved handing as many flyers out as possible and chatting to people about what Dawn Patrol was doing in town. I wondered how Jem would deal with the inevitable pitiful response.

As two-thirds of the team set off to round up potential players, I managed to find an indispensable job at the net, making "essential" adjustments to height and tension. I thought about Karen's prayer again. With real mission activities looming, the "roaring lion" in me wanted to retreat into his cave.

I had hoped that Matt would hang around at the net with me but to my surprise he wandered off, alone, towards a group of girls and lads in their late teens. I watched him introduce himself and hand each of them a flyer. I watched them react. They seemed interested and began to ask him questions. He turned and pointed towards the net.

They laughed and waved him away. I guessed they didn't fancy volleyball. I was struck by the fact that they hadn't dismissed the invitation outright. They were laughing with Matt and not at him. He'd made a good impression.

I pondered his approach for a moment. He had clearly decided to throw himself in and the result didn't look too painful. I wondered whether, by the end of the afternoon, I could make myself do something similar. What was the worst that could happen? I was already wearing the yellow t-shirt after all.

To my immense surprise volleyball was in serious demand that afternoon. It was so popular that, even after we had a full league of teams, groups of friends were sending slightly nervous spokespeople over to ask if they could join in as well.

I was amazed. I'd been certain the whole beach would look at us and think: "Christians on a mission! Keep clear!"

I had been wrong.

As the teams formed, I realised that no one knew we were Christians or, even if they did, no one seemed to be put off. All that they saw was the volleyball net and guys in yellow t-shirts asking if anyone wanted to play. We hadn't been labelled as crazy: conversely, we'd been accepted as providers of high-quality, in-demand beach entertainment. There was no need for me to be afraid or embarrassed. In fact, for the first time I even saw the possibility that I could relax and enjoy the afternoon. Things were beginning to change. I was beginning to change.

The first volleyball match kicked off. A group of shaven-headed lads from Hull played members of an under-21 soccer team from Wokingham. I was grateful for Steve, our semi-professional football player who, as referee, enforced the rules without mercy and who turned out to be brilliant at diffusing tensions before things got out of hand.

The lads from Hull lost. The players shook hands and, as new teams came on court, I was surprised to find that a couple of the lads stuck around to chat to Kate and Alison. I stood close by and eavesdropped on their conversation. The boys asked what the volleyball was all about. The girls were relaxed and friendly as they told the lads about the mission. The boys nodded thoughtfully and took flyers, asking if we would be back the next day with the net.

Post-match chats like this went on all afternoon. God, Jesus, church and Christianity were all mentioned in abundance and no one ran away screaming, burst out laughing, started a fight or did anything even remotely negative. Instead the volleyball/God combination was proving to be a bit of a magnet and a palpably positive atmosphere hung over the court. It was as if we had set up a temporary spiritual drop-in station that people on the beach were comfortable having in their midst and which some decided to make use of.

I watched conversations develop naturally, and when they ended there were smiles and a sense that something worthwhile had taken place. If mission could be like that then I could do it. I wanted to do it. The relaxed vibe and the casual conversations made sense.

The popularity of the volleyball and the ease of the many conversations caused me to wonder where I'd got the impression that doing mission was about telling people who didn't want to listen what you thought was best for their souls. This mission – Dawn Patrol – was about as far from that as it was possible to get. The team members listened as well as talked. There was mutual respect. I liked that.

I had arrived in Newquay convinced that most people had little time for Jesus, even less for Christians and none whatsoever for Christians who wanted to talk about Jesus. As Jem, Steve,

Kate, Alison, Matt and the other team members chatted to assorted volleyball players, my preconceptions crumbled like dusty mortar in an old brick wall. The people on the beach that day obviously had an appetite for spiritual talk and the members of the beach team were doing a good job of whetting it.

Our afternoon's activities began to draw to a close. As for my own part: I had played volleyball, caught the sun and relaxed a whole lot about being part of the mission but, apart from the odd "Hi", I hadn't really spoken to anyone other than my teammates. Ordinarily this would have been fine but, since I had made a decision that morning to try and put some effort into the mission, I felt as if I should have at least exchanged a few words over flyers, or at least over one! As it happened I hadn't handed out even a single flyer.

Perhaps I should have been trying harder to strike up conversation? Then again, surely, I told myself, if it didn't happen, it didn't happen. You can't force a conversation, I reasoned. Conversations need to occur naturally. Anything else is pointless and embarrassing.

I set off for a short walk. Perhaps I'd been in the wrong spot all afternoon. Had I played it too safe? If I did a quick loop of the beach before we packed away, maybe I'd end up talking to someone about God and I'd get myself over my anxiety hump. I stuffed some flyers into my pocket and set off.

The edge of the sea was crammed with children splashing and fighting, mums and dads dangling babies' legs in the water and skinny students tumbling around on bogie-boards. My feet sank into the damp sand as I prowled past the hullabaloo. All the while I was asking God to guide me to the right person. I wanted divine guidance so that if I approached someone, I could be sure that I wasn't going to be dismissed out of hand.

I walked past plenty of people but nothing obvious happened. There was no sign that I should go and speak to any of them. I don't know what kind of sign I was expecting exactly. Perhaps if someone could stop me and say: "Hi! I think you've got something to tell me about God?"

I fumbled with the flyers in my pocket. I wanted God to make it as easy and as obvious as possible for me to talk to someone. If I was going to talk to strangers I wanted guarantees.

I turned so that my walk would take me in a large loop back to where I started and kept praying.

There was no answer.

I persisted: "Just draw my attention to someone, Lord. Make someone obvious. . ."

I was certain that there must be someone on the beach that I could speak to. God simply needed to point out that person. Once he'd done it, he would have proved himself to me by including me in something out of the ordinary. I would be over my worries and could feel like I was a proper part of the mission.

But it didn't happen.

In fact, nothing happened.

God kept quiet and so did I.

My walk took me back to where the volleyball net was being taken down by the rest of the team. I helped to pack away in silence, tangled in my own thoughts like a fish flapping in a net.

As we finished I realised that Matt was not among the group. I scanned the beach for a yellow t-shirt and quickly spotted him a little way off. He was sitting on the sand beside an enormous guy who was turning a green Frisbee over and over in his hands. They were deep in conversation. How come Matt could find someone to chat to – to make it worth his while being on the mission – and I couldn't? How had Matt's conversation started?

Perhaps Matt had simply given the guy a flyer and they'd started chatting. Perhaps calmly handing out a few flyers and being myself was what I should have done rather than striding foolishly round the beach looking for someone to collar while demanding that God prove himself to me. I realised with horror that what I had just tried to do was exactly what I'd been afraid of doing when I arrived in Newquay. What made it worse was that no one else on my team had done anything like it and there had been no need for me to either.

I felt stupid.

I hung behind the team as they left the beach. Matt caught up with me just as I mounted the steps up the cliff.

"Who was that?" I asked, sounding like a jealous girlfriend.

"He's a squaddie," Matt replied brightly, as if chatting about Jesus to soldiers was something he did all the time.

"What did you talk about?" I enquired, continuing the jealous girlfriend theme.

"What he does. His girlfriend. He's on leave so they've come on holiday."

We were nearing the top of the steps. I had to stand to one side to avoid a family coming down so I just nodded. Matt continued:

"He used to go to church when he was younger but he hasn't been for years. He asked me why I bothered going."

"What did you say?" We reached the top of the steps and I stopped.

"I told him that sometimes church can be a bit messed up."

"What did he say to that?"

"He agreed with me." Matt shrugged. "He said he thought about God a lot but he didn't like church. So I asked him if he ever prayed."

"And did he?" I asked, impressed.

"Yeah. He's been out in the Gulf. He said that out there everyone prays even if they won't admit it."

"How long's he been back?" I asked.

"A while. He said that when he was over there being alive got really important and when you can't ask anyone else, you ask God to keep things ticking over safely."

I knew Matt well enough to know that this would have struck a chord with him. He'd been involved with some dodgy characters a few years back and someone had made threats on his life. A small tattoo on his arm was a daily reminder of a past he'd been glad to leave in one piece. Matt knew about asking God to keep him safe against the odds when no one else could help.

"He said he might come to the club night," Matt added.

The rest of the team had moved on ahead so we were standing on our own at the top of the steps in the late afternoon sun. I slapped Matt warmly on the shoulder.

Together we looked over the metal rail and picked out the soldier sitting beside his girlfriend on the sand below. Perhaps he was telling her what he'd been talking about with Matt. He wasn't someone that many people would pick out for a conversation about God. But then neither were many of the people who had played volleyball with us that afternoon. Neither were any of the team. For that matter, neither was I.

I thought about Jesus hanging out with all the least obvious people and how, almost everywhere he went crowds followed, eager to hear what he had to say. I realised that I needed to change what I imagined people thought about God. A relationship with God is not some irrelevance that I was part of peddling at the cynical majority. Everyone has the potential to desire a relationship with God because everyone has a soul that searches for him, even if they are often too distracted by other things to realise it.

A White Witch

The evening began and the next challenge presented itself.

Matt and I were asked to set up a set of decks outside a church on Newquay's busy high street and play to the passing crowds. This was the brainchild of Dawn Patrol's constantly creative organiser, Andy Frost. He wanted to drum up a good vibe, draw people into a coffee bar in the church and generally prompt people to stop and ask questions. Matt and I were a little concerned that putting the decks outside the front of a church might look a bit cheesy and could backfire on the mission. Nevertheless, Andy was the organiser and we agreed. I knew that what we were about to attempt could go either way and hoped our efforts would be well received.

We set the decks up immediately outside the front doors of the United Reformed church. Instantly they began to draw serious attention. The turntables and two very large speakers jostled for space on top of a creaking table. As people passed, engrossed in fish and chips or carrying bags stuffed with cans of lager, scores of eyes flowed from the decks, to Matt and me, then up to the church, and back to the decks. Confusion swam across faces as people tried to compute what might be going on. We just smiled and tried to look normal. Everyone was used to seeing weird things in Newquay but perhaps a set of decks outside the front of a church was a step too far.

We finished setting up and Andy appeared in the church doorway.

"How's it going?" he asked with a hint of nervousness in his voice that made me think he was not as confident about his brainwave as he had seemed ten minutes before.

"We're pretty much ready," I replied. "When do you want us to start?"

Matt was under the table plugging the decks in. Andy scanned the passing crowds and chewed his bottom lip before giving me an answer.

"I thought we'd get some guys to hand out free cans of Coke and flyers while you're playing so maybe wait till they're out then go for it?"

He raised his eyebrows as if he wanted to know whether I thought the open-air-decks plan was a good one or not. I didn't know. Part of me was up for it – the part that was trying hard to be more like a roaring lion than a frightened mouse. Having never DJ'd anywhere remotely similar, I wondered what kind of reception we'd get. I'd soon find out.

While Matt and I waited for the guys to show with the flyers and free Cokes, we flicked through each other's record boxes and compared tunes. We soon began to drum up real excitement between the pair of us, pulling out at least thirty real blinders that just *had* to get played. The plan was that once we'd started we would swap over after every couple of mixes to keep the vibe fresh and thumping. I was beginning to look forward to what was coming.

As we stacked up our records Matt told me about something that the guys in his church at Crawley were doing. For the past six months they had been using decks in their worship. Interested, I asked him how it was working out. Matt began to tell me how he'd not only got heavily involved but really excited. Church had begun to be something he felt part of in a new way. It was becoming a place where he felt he really belonged – somewhere that his love of dance music and DJing could be expressed instead of put on pause. It wasn't a feeling he'd associated with church before. I did a quick mental comparison with my own recent church experience and realised that what was happening in Crawley must be at the root of Matt's surprisingly high level of enthusiasm.

A dozen Dawn Patrollers arriving interrupted

our chat. They began to break open boxes full of cans of Coke and fill their pockets with flyers for the Dawn Patrol club night.

Everything was set. Matt cued up his first tune, grinned across the turntables at me and pressed his thumb down on the *start* button. A massive garage anthem tumbled out of the speakers and bowled into the passing stream of people. Immediate animated recognition burst from almost everyone in the street as the first bars sloshed off the walls of the shops opposite the church, turning every head and bringing several nods of approval.

The Coke-bearing Dawn Patrollers fanned out and began to press free cans into slightly confused, but nevertheless willing, hands. On Fistral beach people were used to thumping music and being offered all kinds of promotional freebies, but outside a church was different. Free Coke and decent tunes outside church was something new but "hey!" you could almost see people thinking, "It's free and it sounds good so who cares?"

Matt and I alternated on the decks and kept the tunes rolling into the street like bowling balls, bringing our corner of Newquay to life. Many of the passing people looked at us with curious fascination and nodded their heads in time with the beats.

A group of lads in their late teens strolled over. They stood around the table, Burberry baseball caps perched on the back of their heads, eyes like excited Jack Russells darting all over the equipment. As they arrived I was going into a mix. The beats from the two tunes rolled sweetly into each other. I flicked at the cross fader, cutting back and forth between the two tunes and sending the whole group into a frenzy of head-ducking excitement.

"*Yes* mate!" several of them yelled as their hands punched into the air and sliced to and fro, tracing the beats.

As I finished the mix and prepared for the next one, the lads barraged Matt with questions about who we were and where we got our tunes and what we were doing on the street outside a church.

He explained and added that God was well into garage. They thought that was hilarious. "Wasn't God into old school stuff?" they joked.

Overall their reaction was positive. Quiet nods, some slight confusion, but from a couple, real curiosity. These two slipped in some carefully worded questions about our connection with church. They listened as Matt gave brief, well-pitched answers. Then, as quickly as they had arrived, the whole group were on their way. They snatched at flyers for the club night and darted away into town promising loudly that they'd be there if the tunes were going to be decent.

The sun dropped below the horizon taking families and older folks with it. They were replaced by a high-energy surge of clubbers heading enmasse towards the town's nightspots.

The street began to resemble a crowded tropical fish tank. Girls and lads of all shapes and sizes were pushing along in both directions, yelling and screeching and swigging from cans and bottles. Some of the more drunk passers-by stopped to dance. Their mates laughed until they'd seen the stupid moves one time too many and yanked them on to the next bar.

I began to wonder if we should pack the decks away. Opportunities for any kind of worthwhile conversations arising from having the decks on the street looked increasingly unlikely. I mentioned my thoughts to a couple of Dawn Patrollers standing close by but they reckoned it was worth sticking around for a while longer. The music was keeping them inspired to approach people with flyers and anyway, they told me, not everyone was completely wasted and someone might come along who needed to talk.

Little did I know that within minutes, that

someone would indeed arrive and she was to give our presence on the street a dramatic focus.

Matt pulled his headphones away from his ears and shouted for a cup of tea. I ducked into the church to fetch it for him. If I had known what would kick off on the street while I was inside, I might have been quicker.

The interior of the church was a wood-panelled oasis of calm. A group of Dawn Patrollers were standing in the vestry laughing with two young homeless guys whose bodies looked as if they had been swallowed by a jumble of dirty black and khaki layers. Bundled-up sleeping bags were slumped patiently at their feet like fat, stained dogs. They slurped tea from cups that looked abnormally vivid and delicate in their grainy fingers. Although they seemed happy enough to be chatting away, they stood awkwardly as if they were half-thinking about making a break for the door. The young Dawn Patrollers who had welcomed them with tea and smiles almost glowed with naïve freshness in comparison.

Through the glass doors that led into the pewless main part of the church I counted eight people. A girl was sitting cross-legged on top of a covered piano absorbed in strumming a guitar. Others were deep in conversations at tables that were dotted around like lily pads on a garden pond. A large man wearing an Iron Maiden t-shirt was playing pool on his own. His long, greasy hair was pulled into a thin ponytail that lay down his back like a dead adder.

I nodded at the group in the vestry. A tall, blonde girl with an open, bright face broke away from the conversation and offered me a cup of tea. I asked if she could make it two. As we waited for the kettle to boil I commented on the peaceful atmosphere. She fiddled with milk and cups and told me that there was a prayer room in the basement.

I raised both eyebrows inquisitively. I hadn't known anything about this but I was seriously encouraged. She continued, telling me that there was a decent sized gathering below us praying constantly for what was going on in and around the church.

That made massive sense. The results were glaring. God was around. The positive reception Matt and I had got with the music had been the result of constant, real-time prayer. I grabbed the teas and hurried back out onto the street, excited about telling Matt that we were plugged into a prayer generator in the basement. However, I emerged from the church straight into a blaring argument that was in full swing beside the decks. My news for Matt would have to wait.

A conversation I'd noticed earlier between three people had erupted. A woman, who had striking features and long dark hair gestured aggressively as she slammed down questions like a wrestler. An enthusiastic Dawn Patroller named JT tried to stay calm but the few replies he was able to fling in the woman's direction were bouncing off unheard.

The woman's boyfriend, wearing an expression that swung continually between amusement and confusion, kept silent and frequently looked away from the conversation at the passing clubbers. He was obviously keen to get going but at that moment he had no chance.

Matt, still busily mixing the tunes, turned his head towards me and mouthed the word "Pray".

I nodded and looked back at the argument. None of the passing clubbers was paying it much attention. The road was noisy; most people had been drinking heavily and were focused on their own group of friends, trying to make it to the next club or bar.

I put the cups of tea down, leant against a wall and, standing a little way from the church doors I began to pray silently, asking God to be part of the conversation.

Other Dawn Patrollers, returning from handing out flyers around the town gathered around. I noticed that Paul was among them – back from DJing elsewhere.

He stood close to the argument and checked out what was going on. He spotted me, flashed me an enquiring glance and nodded towards the couple. I mouthed "Pray" as Matt had done to me a moment before. He nodded back before turning and disappearing into the church with his record box.

I was finding it difficult to pray with so much going on around me so I kept my words simple. I simply asked God to help JT to know what to say that might penetrate the young woman's armour-plated exterior.

Paul reappeared in the doorway of the church minus his record box. The woman was insisting loudly enough for me to hear that the Bible was a bunch of made-up lies and that JT was wasting his time trying to talk to anyone about it. JT tried to give an answer but he was shouted down with another blunt statement. Paul chose that moment to head straight into the fray.

～

The young woman was not fazed by his presence. In fact, when she realised that Paul was with JT she seemed almost pleased to have another Christian to dish out a verbal battering to.

Paul jabbed into the conversation with one or two quietly spoken comments. He sidestepped an aggressive retort and countered immediately with confidence. As he spoke, he stretched his palms out as if to demonstrate the commonsense obviousness of his remarks. Surprisingly he was allowed to finish and continue. I guessed he had followed through with a couple of well-chosen theological head-shots.

JT stepped back. He looked exhausted and relieved. It reminded me of a tag-team wrestle. Paul had stepped into the ring to do theological battle with a female Hulk Hogan. His gaze was locked onto the young woman's who had now shifted not only her attention but also her posture towards him. The boyfriend continued to hover as a passive observer, ignored by them both.

They argued for a long time. Every Dawn Patroller within a hundred metres was aware of the battle and had been asked to pray hard. Some had tried to chip in but it was no use. The struggle was between Paul and the young woman. The rest of us had to leave them to it. The best way any of us could help was to keep praying. Everyone wondered how things would end up.

It was late. Matt and I exhausted our supply of records. We decided to pack the decks away. We worked quickly and the equipment was soon heading safely into the church.

The trestle table was left behind and as I returned to collapse it, proceedings between Paul and the young woman took a swift and surprising turn. Her voice dropped, along with the aggressive arm gestures, and gave way to a subdued dialogue. I kept still, crouched over the folded table, absorbed in the gripping scene. I could only wonder what had happened for such a sudden and obvious change to occur.

Paul said something and as the young woman replied her boyfriend began to laugh. She glared at him disdainfully and pushed him hard in the chest. He looked shocked. Paul didn't look up. He kept his focus on the young woman. More words were exchanged and then something happened that gripped and stunned me. Paul and the young woman bowed their heads in what was obviously a prayer.

I couldn't hear what Paul prayed but his words flowed for half a minute. As he finished the woman's manner changed. Stillness settled on her face. Her shoulders seemed to drop slightly. She looked attentively at Paul for a moment with elusive curiosity. And then it was finished. She turned and disappeared into the busy night with her boyfriend.

Paul turned towards the church. The exhaustion was obvious on his face. Several Dawn Patrollers converged on him at once, full of questions. As he was ushered inside I followed, dragging the trestle table. Everyone wanted the full story.

Paul shook his head and puffed his cheeks again and again. He looked as if he had simply run out of words. After almost two hours of wrestling – both verbally and spiritually – there was nothing else he could bring himself to say. He had had an epic encounter and he needed to slump quietly in a corner and recharge.

Someone suggested that we pray for Paul. He was spiritually as well as mentally and physically exhausted. Prayer was essential.

A group of us gathered round. Some put their hands on Paul's tired arms and shoulders. He closed his eyes and sat silently as we asked God to give him back his strength and energy, to protect him and encourage him. We also asked God to use what Paul had said to make a difference to the lives of the young woman and her boyfriend.

In the early hours of the next morning, back in the quiet of the girls' room at the NCC, the members of the beach team sat around with Jem and Paul discussing the evening's events. Despite everyone's complete exhaustion after a long day, there was a buzz of excitement.

Paul had regained the power of speech and began to answer our stream of questions. Jem laughed in disbelief as we filled him in on what had happened and kept saying he wished he'd been there to see it all.

The young woman, Paul explained, was a white witch. She lived with another, older witch in a flat above one of the shops opposite the church where we'd been DJing. She and her flatmate knew about the mission and had been casting spells against our work in the town. She had told Paul that Christians were a negative and oppressive presence in the town and she'd asked him why we didn't just leave people alone.

We listened patiently to Paul but what the whole team really wanted to know was what had happened to bring about such a sudden and dramatic change in events. How had Paul been enabled so suddenly to pray with her?

He told us that he had asked her what she did for fun. Did she take drugs or get drunk? She had said no, she never touched drugs or alcohol because they made her more miserable than she already was. It was this that her boyfriend had laughed at. He had clearly had no idea that she was miserable.

Paul had ventured to tell her that he knew how she felt – he had felt the same until a couple of years before. He'd gone on to explain how a simple but profound experience had sparked his faith in Jesus. Jesus was real, he had told her, and, far from being oppressive or negative, he was *really* able to make a positive difference.

While he'd been engaged in his conversation with this white witch, our prayers for guidance and courage had been working. Paul could recognise their effect because once he'd talked about his own experience the young woman seemed to listen in a new way. Sensing that the conversation was drawing to a close, Paul had decided to take a risk and offered to pray for her.

Almost half the team had been watching and had seen the effect of that prayer. Something unmistakable and profound had happened. God had touched the young woman in a way she had never known. In doing that, he had also touched every Dawn Patroller watching.

This incident particularly affected me. Watching Paul being courageous enough to offer to pray for the woman after being on the receiving end of almost two hours of aggression was powerful enough in itself. But to witness a physical change as a peace that she didn't understand washed over her – that knocked any remaining doubts I might have had well and truly on the head. God was on that street and he had been in the middle of that conversation. I had no doubt that he had used the encounter to begin something life-changing in the young woman's life. In fact he had used the encounter to do something life-changing in all of our lives – even the team members who had missed the action and who merely heard about it afterwards.

Faith and excitement bubbled up inside my tired body like a washing machine going into rinse cycle. I needed to go to bed but felt too wired to sleep. I knew that awesome things were possible in what remained of the week and I was desperate, not only to see more, but also to do more. Matt had spoken to the soldier on the beach; Paul had had an awesome encounter with a white witch. I wanted to go next.

God in the Club

"Get the music back on!"

The guy standing beside me on the sweaty

dance floor was not impressed that the DJ had just allowed the last tune to play out without mixing it. People around him joined in:

"What's going on?"

"Sort it out!"

"Is this a raid or what?"

After four days of volleyball, handing out flyers, meeting new people and gradually learning to trust God, Thursday evening had arrived and the Dawn Patrol event at Fosters nightclub was well under way. Music had been thundering out across the undulating sea of heads that packed the dance floor but now there was only the hum of the crowd.

Someone on the stage began speaking into a microphone but it was difficult to hear what was being said over the heckling from the dance floor. The club was dark. I had to strain to see who was speaking. It was Jem. He was appealing for quiet. I wondered what was happening. Was someone hurt?

"Sorry!" he shouted. "But I've got something really important to say."

A few people continued heckling but most were probably wondering what Jem would come out with.

"This is going to sound a bit strange to a lot of

people," he continued. "But I believe God has just told me something really important about someone here tonight."

Now he had everyone's full attention.

"A few minutes ago God put a picture in my head of a young woman sitting on the edge of her bed in a room that was painted pink."

People looked around at each other as if they were expecting someone to put their hand up and say it was them.

"It's someone here tonight," Jem motioned with a hand at the crowd. "You were sitting alone and crying and feeling that no one could help you. I think perhaps you've just found out that you're pregnant and maybe you've been making arrangements to have an abortion but you're confused and you don't know what to do."

This was incredible! If Jem was right and the woman was in the club, right at that moment I guess she would be freaking out. No one would have arrived that evening expecting God to speak to them like that. Jem carried on.

"If that person is you, come and find me. I'll be in the cloakroom – we've made it into a prayer room for tonight – and I'll be there for the rest of the evening. We can talk and maybe try and help. Thanks."

70

Jem jumped down from the stage and the music kicked back on. I took a deep breath, probably along with most of the people in the club. Everyone would be asking themselves if Jem had got it right. Would the girl show up in the prayer room? We could only wait and see.

As I thought about Jem's words and how amazing it would be if he turned out to be right, my mind flicked back two hours, to the minutes before we had opened the club's doors. I recalled the image of fifty Dawn Patrollers standing in a circle on the dance floor calling out to God, asking him to show up that evening. A holy babble of voices – everyone praying at once with passion and excitement. We had assured God that he was welcome in the club. We asked him to impact everyone who came through the doors – including the security and bar staff.

I looked around the club. The people had come. The place was buzzing. The music had been blinding and loads of people were dancing. Conversations between Dawn Patrollers and people they had invited were a big part of the night too. It was going really well.

Just then I spotted Paul in the DJ booth. I climbed in to join him. He was playing next and was thumbing through his tightly packed record box, selecting tunes for his set. As we chatted, Andy Frost stuck his smiling head over the edge of the booth, motioned to me and then, yelling in my ear, asked if I could announce the start of the break-dance competition. He jabbed at the microphone with his finger. As Paul prepared to take over on the decks, I made the announcement. The break-dance comp was imminent.

I looked down at the dance floor and noticed a large clearing appearing in the centre. I gave it my full attention. Dancing bodies were fanning out-wards. Then I spotted them. On their knees among the crowd, Andy and three other Dawn Patrollers were carefully unrolling a large sheet of lino. It would form a decent surface for the breakers to dance on.

Paul cued up his first tune. The fast beats of the previous DJ's thumping house track were reaching a crescendo. As the lino reached its full length, Andy and the guys stood up and Paul zipped the cross fader across. Speeding beats morphed into a laid back rolling break beat.

The crowd liked the change and responded with enthusiasm. The movements of everyone in the place altered instantly. A calmer vibe hit the dance floor accompanied by a ripple of expectation.

The breakers emerged from the crowd, which

packed round in a tight formation. People strained to see between and over the heads of others. The beats started to pick up and Paul began to work his magic on the cross fader, scratching and cutting between hip-hop and classic soul tracks.

The breakers did their thing. The crowd roared with approval. The moves got crazy. Legs spun all over the place. At one point the atmosphere got so hyped that Paul could not contain himself any longer. He jumped down from the DJ booth, leaving his records spinning unattended, and body-popped his way around the lino blasting the crowd into a frenzy. It was wild. I couldn't even break but I was tempted to jump in the ring and give it a go because I was so excited.

Eventually Andy took to the stage to announce a winner and hand over prizes. A fresh DJ was in the booth, poised with his tunes ready to go, but before Andy handed over to him, he offered a reminder of something that had been mentioned over the microphone several times that night already.

"Just a reminder. . . We've set up a prayer room in the cloakroom people," he announced.

"We believe in a God who answers prayer," he smiled. "A God who wants to heal people. A God who wants you to know him."

No one heckled. I was amazed.

"If you want to get prayed for – for anything at all – get to the prayer room and there will be someone there to pray with you. Cheers."

With that, he gave a thumbs up to the DJ and disappeared into the crowd as a thumping drum and bass track exploded across the dance floor.

I immediately decided to go and check out the prayer room. I wanted to see if anyone was making use of it. I also badly wanted to find out if the girl Jem had described had showed up.

I waded across the leaping bodies on the dance floor. Sweat from frantically nodding heads slapped into my ducking face. At the other side of the dance floor was the bar. I made my way along it in the direction of the prayer room.

I wasn't expecting to find too much going on when I got there. Which is why the sight that greeted me at the prayer room doors almost knocked me over.

There was a queue. To get into a prayer room! In a nightclub!

I laughed out loud. This was amazing. In my wildest expectations of the event, I had not dreamed that the prayer room would ever be occupied by more than two or three faithful Dawn Patrollers who were looking forward to getting out and having a dance. But far, far, far from that, here were people wanting, volunteering, even needing to pray. It was crazy.

But this was what the week had been building towards. All the prayer and worship and conversations and handing out flyers were partly aimed at getting people to come together in a place where they could experience God.

And God had definitely showed up. I could sense the Holy Spirit in the building and as I looked at the people around me I knew that we could all feel it. It felt as if we were part of some kind of very large, electric family in a house where something serious was brewing. No one was quite sure exactly what it was that was brewing but we all knew it was going to be pretty good. Even the security guys had picked up on it. It was clear in their slightly bewildered but surprisingly calm faces.

The music stopped again. There was the usual heckling and then a voice on the microphone that I recognised. I bobbed my head and stood on tip-toes to see who it was.

Paul!

Sporadic heckling continued but not loudly enough to drown Paul out. He announced that he had something to say. He promised he would be quick. I wondered if he was going to add to what Jem had said earlier.

"Get off!" yelled the guy next to me. Paul continued, undeterred.

"Weed. . . Coke. . . E. . . Speed. . ." Paul pronounced the names of these drugs deliberately and with conviction.

A shout of approval went up from a couple of groups on the dance floor.

"I used to live for getting high," continued Paul. "But I was an idiot. . ." He tapped the side of his head with his forefinger.

He began to mention Jesus. Andy Frost had previously asked for a few volunteers to stand up and say something about their faith throughout the evening. Paul had obviously agreed to do so.

He spoke for less than two minutes: just long enough to say something about the God he believed in; hopefully just long enough to make an impact. As he climbed down from the stage the enormous thump of the bass bins kicked out across the dance floor as the DJ started the music again. There was rapturous applause although I wasn't sure if it was for the tune or Paul.

I hoped it was partly for Paul. I was under no illusions about the amount of guts it must have taken for him to stand up and tell a packed nightclub that Jesus had sorted his life out. Neither of us knew it at that moment but a couple of hours later Paul would be repeating the words he had just spoken and I would be adding many of my own when we met a young guy who was hoping to score some weed.

The music was off. It was after 2am. Records were packed away and people slowly left the club, many deep in conversation. There was a unity and quiet exhilaration in the air that you could almost taste. I took all of this in, enjoying the atmosphere and the energy but a question was burning in my mind: what about the pregnant girl whom Jem had described? Had she showed up? Had he got it right?

I made a quick search of the groups sitting and standing around the car park; no one seemed in any hurry to leave and go to bed. There was no sign of Jem. I found Paul and Alison and asked if they knew what had happened with the girl. They didn't.

Suddenly we spotted Jem. He was leaving the club with one of the doormen. They were laughing together. As they emerged into the warm night the three of us called Jem over.

"What a mental night!" he burst out as he strode over in his three-quarter-length trousers. The three of us had to agree.

"Did that girl God told you about show up?" chirped Alison. "The one in the pink room?"

Jem nodded enthusiastically.

"Yep!"

My mouth dropped open slightly. Paul grinned from ear to ear. Alison laughed out loud.

"God's amazing!" she announced.

Jem nodded in agreement.

"So what happened?" Alison rolled her hands over each other impatiently. "Come on. . ."

Jem began to tell us how the girl had waited until the evening was almost over before she had had the courage to go to the prayer room and find someone to speak to about what he had said.

He and a couple of female Dawn Patrollers had sat with her for the final half an hour, in a corner of the busy prayer room, listening to her story.

What God had told Jem was spot on. She had recently discovered she was pregnant but had an unsupportive family and no money. She had booked an abortion earlier that week and had been in an emotional mess ever since. She had spent hours crying her heart out in her bedroom – which was indeed painted pink!

Amazingly, she had been handed a flyer in the street during the week and at the last minute she'd decided to come to the club night because the

Dawn Patroller she'd met had been friendly and she had nowhere else to go. Little would that Dawn Patroller have realised how God was going to use a simple flyer to impact two lives.

As they had talked and prayed together, she told them that she wanted to change her mind about the abortion. This was such great news. The young woman and the tiny life growing inside her needed support, care, attention and friends. God had seen her tears and listened to her cries for help and had stepped in and directed her to the right place. Things would work out well for her and the baby. Jem and the girls had swapped contact details with this young woman and were going to be staying in touch.

Beaming all across his face as he finished telling us, Jem suggested that we hit the twenty-four-hour garage for microwave pasties.

"I'm starving!" he yelled, patting his belly.

It was a good plan. I was pretty hungry myself. The night had been a long one and pasties sounded very good indeed.

Little did we know as we headed towards the bright lights of the garage that our night had barely begun.

God on the Street

We were ambling away from the twenty-four-hour garage, eagerly shoving microwave pasties into our mouths, when I noticed a guy with a shaved head striding confidently towards me. I sidestepped to let him pass but he stopped abruptly, as if inspiration had just landed on his head, and dropped an unexpected question.

"Any of you lot got a spliff you can sort me out with?"

Jem returned the broad smile. The slim man was younger than I had first thought – late teens at a guess. He was dressed in a camouflage jacket and low-slung jeans and was now looking round eagerly, I supposed for the spliff to materialise. Alison and Paul were just behind us and had caught up but were looking blank. They hadn't heard his question.

Paul leant forward into what was almost a huddle between Jem, myself and our new friend, and asked inquisitively what was up. As he did so I noticed a thickly packed record bag slung over our new friend's shoulder.

"A *spliff*. . . I was asking if anyone's got a spliff to help a needy DJ?" He laughed as he emphasised the word needy, as if we all shared some kind of universal understanding that sometimes only a spliff would do the trick.

"Tonight's been a bit of a mad one and I'm gagging for a smoke," he continued. "Come on. . . surely one of you must have a crumb of gear and a couple of skins for a man in need?" He was smiling warmly, expectantly.

As he finished speaking, a drunken chorus from a slowly approaching group of lads rolled through the air. I looked up as one of them tripped and landed on the road with a nasty slap. Fortunately for him there weren't too many cars on the streets of Newquay at 3am. His mates collapsed laughing as he struggled to his knees and loudly mourned the loss of his kebab – now strewn across the ground. I pulled my attention back to our little huddle and caught the eye of our new friend.

"Sorry mate," I offered sympathetically. "We haven't got any gear."

"*Pleease*," he grinned, opening his hands in a friendly, mock-begging gesture.

"Just a little bit. You wouldn't even notice."

All of us laughed, including him.

"Seriously mate," I continued, "None of us smoke."

He didn't look convinced but shrugged his

shoulders with an understanding smile and prepared to move on. He hoisted the bag of records further up onto his shoulder. Paul and Alison moved aside to let him pass. He shifted beyond us, taking backward steps, thanking us for stopping and enthusiastically wishing us a good night. As he began to move away I had a bizarre urge to say something to him about God. I was fired up from the week's events and especially after what had just happened with the pregnant girl at the club.

My mind was rolling through a story from the Bible where Peter and John, two of Jesus' closest mates, bumped into a paraplegic guy on their way to the temple. The guy asked them if they could help him out with some loose change and Peter delivered a classic reply along the lines of: "We're a bit skint at the moment mate, but if you want to walk again then get up on your feet in the name of Jesus!"

With Peter's radical response swelling in my head, I figured that there was nothing to lose if I did something mildly similar. After all, if the DJ was relaxed enough to stop four strangers in the street and ask for a spliff, then surely I could mention Jesus without worrying about it? I held my hand up to stop him and, without waiting for another thought to distract me, I said:

"None of us can give you a spliff but we can tell you about Jesus."

As the words left my mouth, I wondered what I was thinking. But there it was. The words had been spoken and the statement hung in the Newquay morning air like a clumsily thrown beach ball. I could sense that my three companions couldn't believe it either. The four of us looked at the DJ and he looked back at us steadily. Within an instant he replied:

"Go on then. . . Tell me about Jesus." There wasn't even a hint of sarcasm in his voice. He was serious.

Here we were, on the streets of Newquay at 3am. . . A spliff-seeking DJ had just said; "Tell me about Jesus!" to four Christians who were supposedly there to do exactly that.

Appallingly I couldn't think where to begin or what on earth it was that we could tell this guy about Jesus. I hadn't thought that he might say yes; I hadn't imagined he might actually *want* to hear about Jesus. I had assumed that within a few seconds we would be walking away, saying to each other: "Oh well, at least we tried, it's up to God now. . ."

But it wasn't up to God. Well, of course it was mostly up to God, but right then it was also up to us. . . or rather me, since I had started it all and I'd already had a look at the others and seen their slightly shocked faces. So that left me. . . *and God*. I had to come good on my offer and tell this guy something about Jesus right there and then.

Jem broke the silence by asking the guy his name. This was good. It was up to all of us again – not just me and God.

"Adam," he told us. We introduced ourselves and more smiles were exchanged along with plenty of handshaking. I asked him if he knew anything at all about Jesus.

"I think he was a good bloke..." He nodded thoughtfully before adding, in all seriousness; "I think he was probably a bit of a smoker to be honest. . . into chilling out and being peaceful and not harming anyone. I respect all that."

He looked around at our faces to see how we'd react to his ideas. We were nodding thoughtfully.

"He was definitely about peace and not harming others," I replied. "I don't know about smoking weed."

"Why not?" Adam interrupted. "No one knows, do they? Jesus could well have enjoyed a bit of puff. God made marijuana so he must have meant us to smoke it. I can't see the problem myself..."

As he finished speaking, he off-loaded his

record bag onto the pavement between his feet and began rolling his shoulders in relief. I assumed this meant he was happy to stay and talk for at least a little while longer. This was good – I liked him.

Paul thought for a moment before suggesting that Jesus wouldn't have been into smoking dope because he needed to stay focused. Adam shook his head by way of disagreeing.

I could see the marijuana conversation beginning to lead us down a blind alley. The fact that people who smoke a lot of dope often think that everyone else (particularly religious leaders) are big on it too, has always mystified me. Anyhow, we needed to move away from the whole smoking dope thing so I ended it by suggesting that if Jesus and the disciples were passing a bong round every morning after breakfast, they wouldn't have even got out of the house, let alone travelled all over the countryside healing the sick and teaching profound things to vast crowds.

Adam pondered this with an unconvinced expression that was interrupted by yet more rowdy lads who were shouting bizarre things at us, each other and the darkened windows above the local shops. As Adam prepared a reply, three of them linked arms and stampeded towards us, bellowing a football chant. I prepared for them to ram into us as a way of starting a fight but at the last minute they broke company, one of them screamed something incoherent – spraying us with tiny particles of chewed kebab in the process – and then they were off, surging drunkenly up the road to bundle their mates.

The moment they had disappeared, Adam bowled more questions at us, none of which involved cannabis. He seemed genuinely keen to find out why we thought Jesus was worth considering. The conversation crackled and sparked like a firework building to an exciting climax. As Adam suggested ideas about Jesus, the four of us listened carefully and chipped in responses, some of which prompted a nod of agreement, others a frown or a shrug, and others a new line of questions. What Adam couldn't understand was why we were so hung up on Jesus at the expense of other worthy religious teachers.

Between us, over a whole hour and a half, standing in that street, we began to tell Adam that Jesus wasn't just a good teacher but was God himself who had come to earth as a man. Adam stroked his chin, listened carefully and replied with more questions along the lines of: "So if Jesus was God then what about other religions? What about everyone who didn't believe in Jesus, or who had never even heard of Jesus, even if they were good, sincere people? Would God condemn them and send them all to hell? What sort of God was that? Why would we want to know a God like that, let alone talk about him? Why couldn't God just chill out a bit?"

We listened and listened. One by one Alison, Paul and I offered replies to his questions, giving small answers and suggesting ways of thinking about God that were new to him. We used stories and analogies that we had found helpful for our own questions. Alison incessantly emphasised, in her lovely northern lilt, God's massive love for Adam, his intimate knowledge of him, his intense desire for a relationship with him. Paul focused on the need all of us have for something real, not the numb high of a spliff, but the no-come-down peace of God. I chipped in here and there with whatever seemed to fit in the gaps.

Jem said nothing, for the most part, and instead was pacing up and down. I could tell he was praying. Deep, concentrated Spirit-praying. Jem was tuning into God – trying to listen to what he had to say. While the rest of us, including Adam, chucked God-questions and ideas around and chomped on them eagerly as if we were sharing out ten different types of takeaway food, Jem was asking God to give the situation something big and real and beyond words.

Eventually Alison was called away by a friend and Paul agreed to go with her, 4.30am not being the greatest time for walking alone in Newquay. Jem and I were left with Adam.

During the relatively short amount of time we had spent with our new friend, we had covered some pretty deep spiritual ground. I caught myself thinking about friends back in London that I'd known for ten years but with whom I'd barely scratched the surface of the things we'd been talking about with Adam. I guessed this was because often it's easier to talk about deep spiritual stuff with people you've only just met – maybe because neither of you are risking looking stupid in front of someone you'll be seeing again.

We had discussed with Adam who Jesus was, what he did, why he came and where that left us. We had debated other faiths and philosophies and a wedge of doubts, worries and objections to the idea of embarking upon a personal relationship with the God-man: Jesus.

The conversation had been dynamic, good-natured and uplifting but I could sense it drawing to a natural conclusion. There didn't seem to be much more to say about Jesus at that moment and

I didn't want to push the discussion on artificially. I was prepared to shake Adam by the hand, tell him I'd enjoyed meeting him, wish him all the best with his DJing and roll back to my sleeping bag.

As I began to offer Adam my hand, Jem announced something bizarre. In fact, what he said was *so* odd that either he'd completely lost the plot or he was one hundred per cent certain God had supernaturally given him some information about Adam. At that point I couldn't fathom why, if God *had* told Jem anything at all, he'd told him this:

"You've got an accommodation problem haven't you?" The words rolled confidently out of Jem's mouth like an aircraft captain announcing that we were clear for take off.

Adam and I looked at him in silence.

He has? I wondered.

"Er, yes. . ." admitted an astonished Adam whose face looked like he had just seen a ghost but was determined to get a decent explanation.

"How d'you know that?" he asked Jem with a mixture of fear, suspicion and curiosity in his voice.

"You've got a housing problem," continued Jem, "and I think God wants you to know that he's going to sort it."

Adam and I were completely stunned.

Neither of us understood what had just happened or what might need to happen next.

Jem began to explain that he had been asking God to tell him something specific about Adam to help him realise that underneath all of the talking about Jesus was something real and personal.

Feeling as if the three of us had entered some new level of intimacy, I asked Adam what was going on with his living situation.

He explained that he had no money for rent and was going to be evicted later that day. He added that his brother owed him some money. If he could get it from him in time, things might work out.

Jem offered to pray that this would be the case and reassured Adam that even if his brother didn't show with the cash, God could still work things out for him one way or another.

I looked at Adam's face and could see that something important was going on in his head and in his heart. With the supernatural knowledge God had just given Jem, he had blown life into everything that had been said.

"You seriously think God is *actually* bothered about me?" Adam asked with deep gravity in his voice.

"Totally," I replied, nodding.

"And you're telling me you believe he's really fussed about my rent?" he continued.

"*Mate*. . . definitely!" pronounced Jem. "He's only gone and proved it in front of your nose just now!" Jem was properly excited by what he felt God was doing. "And," he continued, "I think you have a choice to make about God right now. . . right here on the street."

None of us spoke for a moment. It felt like the three of us were standing in an eternity-changing moment. Inside Adam a hazy realisation was forming that the things we had said about Jesus were solid, real things. He stared down at the full record bag between his feet, chewing a nail earnestly and mulling over Jem's challenge to ask God to become a part of his life.

In my head I prayed a simple prayer asking God to give all three of us wisdom in what we said and did. I had been praying like this on and off since Adam had first told us his name but now I tried to be more focused. What was happening was too important to mess up.

"OK. . ." Adam looked up, rubbing a hand over his shaved head. "Let's say that God's real and that he knows about me and that for some weird reason he gives a monkeys about my life. What should I do about it?"

"He's real," I assured him, "and he gives a lot more than a monkeys about your life. You know I've got nothing to gain by telling you that. I'm telling you because I know it's true."

It suddenly hit me that I had travelled a long way in my faith since arriving and watching the team litter-picking on the beach a few days previously.

Adam looked into my eyes, silently assessing my words, nodding his head gently and chewing the inside of his lip. I held his gaze which, in another time and place would have been read as aggressive or weird, but right then we both knew it was the best way of showing that what I had told him about God was the truth.

"So, *what*? Do we pray or something?" Adam grinned, looking back and forth at Jem and I.

"Praying is a great plan," replied Jem.

"Well, if God is listening like you say," Adam continued, "and he wants something to do with me, then we can pray. I'm up for whatever..."

I dug my hands deep into my pockets and looked down the deserted street realising for a moment how bizarre but unmissable meeting Adam had been and how shocked my pre-Newquay self would have been to find me having this kind of conversation.

Jem asked Adam if it would be OK if we led him in a prayer asking Jesus to come and be a real part of his life. Adam didn't hesitate for a moment:

"After all that's been said, and then the whole thing with the rent money. . ." he paused and thought for a moment before continuing.

"I have to admit to you that I do feel a bit different... Whether that's God – *Jesus* – or not, I don't know. Maybe it is, maybe it isn't. If it is, and he can sort out my rent I'm interested. The proof's in the pudding yeah? If Jesus comes good for me, I've definitely got some thinking to do. No doubt about it. . ."

"I think he'll sort out your rent situation," Jem assured him. "The way I see it tonight has been Jesus' way of getting your attention. Sometimes it takes a bit of a crisis for us to let him do what he wants to do."

"And what's that then?" Adam enquired swiftly.

"Love us," was Jem's simple but honest answer.

Adam raised his eyebrows to acknowledge the possibility that this statement might have a vague ring of credibility.

"So, are we doing this prayer thing then or what?" he announced in a good-natured but almost impatient tone.

So, at Adam's request, Jem and I led him in a

simple prayer thanking God for everything that had happened that morning and asking Jesus to step into his life and start making a difference. The three of us kept our eyes open. Adam carefully watched us in turn as we spoke to God and then followed with some fumbled but ample words of his own. Jem finished by thanking God that he would be taking care of Adam's accommodation problem. After that the three of us stood silently for a moment taking in all that had happened over almost two hours.

Within a few minutes, we had said heartfelt goodbyes and were going our separate ways into the Newquay morning. Jem and I, buzzing with an almost drug-like excitement, headed back to the sweaty church hall to wake our team up and tell them what had happened. Adam wandered back to his bed-sit, his head no doubt doing overtime as he thought through everything that had happened in reply to his simple request for a spliff.

We had swapped phone numbers and Jem had promised to meet up with Adam again and hook him into a group where he could keep asking questions.

Jem and I had taken a small risk and God had used it to begin proving himself to Adam in a crazy way. We were exhausted but before crashing out, Jem and I made sure to take some time to pray and ask God to protect and grow Adam's new-found but tiny, vulnerable faith.

As I pushed my tired legs into my sleeping bag, my brain faintly registered the fact that less than twenty-four hours of Dawn Patrol remained. It wasn't possible, I thought to myself as I closed my eyes, for much more to happen in the limited time left.

I couldn't have been more wrong!

Father Abraham

"We're going to prayer-walk through the town centre following a guy dragging an eight-foot wooden cross!"

Andy Frost was standing at the front of Newquay Christian Centre's crowded auditorium announcing what we would be doing later that day as a kind of grand finale.

In spite of all that I had experienced in the previous days, Andy's suggestion reminded me of the wave of fear and uncertainty I had felt when I first arrived in town. God had brought me a long way in a short space of time. He had dealt with all kinds of doubts but that didn't stop me from being frown-inducingly daunted at the idea of processing through the busy town centre, in the middle of the day, following someone struggling with a heavy cross. I had stepped outside my comfort zone several times that week but being part of what Andy suggested would be more like taking a long-jump sized run up and jumping out. I could accept that some things were worth doing even if they were likely to make me feel self conscious or even embarrassed. Andy's suggestion however, was in a new and scary league for me. I wondered if it was an unnecessary step too far.

Nevertheless, it had been decided. The prayer-walk was what we were going to do – all seventy of us – and everyone dressed in yellow t-shirts.

We would be praying for the town, *in* the town – preferably out loud, according to Andy. We would be winding our way slowly through the streets – crowded with holidaymakers – towards Fistral beach where we would. . .

Well, no one really seemed too sure about what we would be doing when we arrived at Fistral. But whatever it was, I was certain that it couldn't be as scary as the journey there would be.

The sun beat down on us as we made our way through the town centre. It was just as crowded as I had imagined – in fact, more crowded. People were obliging, though. We were given lots of space. As the yellow column marched at the pace of the young guy dragging the cross, families and old people – in fact everyone within twenty metres – cleared to the sides of the street in a way that reminded me of the biblical story of Moses and the parting of the Red Sea.

I kept smiling. Many of the Dawn Patrollers around me prayed out loud. I felt desperately self-conscious. I gave it a brief shot but realised that I was thinking more about what I might look like than what I was saying. Quickly I decided that silent prayer would have to be good enough.

It was certainly a march of witness. No one could miss seventy yellow-t-shirted young people, most of whom appeared to be talking to them-selves. Or, perhaps more to the point, no one on the high street that afternoon could miss the guy sweating and staggering under the weight of a splinter-packed, hulking wooden cross. It gave a shocking focus to our whole gathering.

Uncomfortable expressions fell over plenty of faces. Some even looked horrified. It struck me that in spite of the various ways in which people might misread or be offended by what they saw, discomfort and disgust were fitting responses to seeing a man dragging a cross through crowded streets under the beating sun. There were people in town that afternoon who were obviously prompted into some serious thinking because of what they had seen.

It made me smile (a small smile) to look at myself. I was voluntarily taking part in something that only a few days earlier I would have been horrified at the mention of. I would have dismissed such a march as a prime example of over-eager Christians doing more harm than good, scaring everyone off with their wacky, cult-like nonsense and embarrassing themselves in the process. However, my sacredness had taken on a new perspective, because there I was, plodding along in my yellow t-shirt feeling surprisingly pleased. I had an opportunity to make a deliberate statement to myself and to God about how things now stood between the two of us.

After what seemed like a very long time indeed – long enough for me to swing between feeling slightly awkward and fairly relaxed several times – we arrived at Fistral beach. We followed Andy, in procession, across the sand, through the ranks of sunbathers. As we flip-flopped past, smiling and chatting among ourselves (the praying had mostly stopped once we hit the beach), I noticed that many of the sunbathers, distracted for a moment from their beers and tanning oil, appeared to be seriously disturbed by our arrival. I couldn't say I blamed them. The sight of us was not something that you saw every day. It would be a talking point.

We picked our way through the crowds and kept walking until we were almost alone – well clear of sunbathers. We stopped on a section of beach that was open and uncluttered and where there was enough space for the seventy of us to form a large circle. A welcome breeze from the sea cooled the back of my legs and neck as I faced in towards my fellow Dawn Patrollers and imagined, along with everyone else, what might happen next.

There were some jokes and a bit of laughter. As we waited I looked around the circle, making eye-contact with various individuals that I'd had the chance to get to know during the week: Matt, Jem, Paul and others. We smiled at each other. Inside me a seed of delight began to swell in my stomach and pulse around my body. It was the kind of feeling that comes from realising that you are among people you have grown to love and who love you back. We'd met less than a week before and yet here were people to whom, at that moment, I felt closer than some of my oldest friends.

This probably had a fair bit to do with being thrown together on a mission where we were way out of our depth. But it wasn't just being chucked together, scared silly and surviving. The closeness I felt with many of the people standing around me on the sand was more than that. It was about some kind of unfathomable unity between us and God.

Everyone standing in that circle loved God. Including me.

That was amazing!

God was amazing!

And so was everyone else!

I was in danger of blissing out there and then so I paused and took a deep breath. As I did so, continuing to grin, somebody announced what we'd be doing next. I registered the words but I couldn't quite believe them.

I looked at Paul who was standing next to me to see if I had heard properly. His face told me everything I needed to know. I laughed out loud.

"They can't be serious?" I offered.

Paul was shaking his head and smiling the kind of smile that says: *I can't believe I've got to do this. . . Let's get it over and done with.*

There on the beach, in full view of hundreds of people, we began to sing that great Sunday school anthem 'Father Abraham had many sons', complete with the whole range of head-nodding, arm shaking, leg-stomping, turning around on the spot actions. It was loud and we looked stupid and there was no hiding.

I'm pretty sure that nobody actually reached the end of the song. By half-way through, at least half of us were doubled over with laughter. By the time three-quarters had been sung, almost everyone had collapsed on the sand in hysterics. It was a welcome release. Our walk to the beach had been headed up by a graphic reminder of the outrageous sacrifice Jesus made for every one of us. It was profound, big stuff. Quite rightly we had taken that part seriously. But singing a kids' song and laughing helplessly together on the sand seemed a fitting way to finish up. God has a sense of humour and he loves it when we have a laugh.

Eventually we climbed to our feet. Andy wanted us to finish by praying together for Newquay and the people we had met during the week.

Around the circle team members began to call out to God. I kept my eyes open and listened and gradually became aware of a feeling beginning to grow inside me. It was an awareness – a recognition of something that was right in front of me – something I had possibly known all week but hadn't paid any attention to. Before I could acknowledge this new and growing awareness properly however, I realised that someone was standing behind me.

I turned around slowly and found myself being faced by not one, but two people: a girl and a guy in their early twenties. They were decked out in baggy linen – much of it orange and were both sporting an impressive amount of dreadlocks. The guy had a wispy beard. He smiled at me and shuffled a little closer.

"Hey!" he offered, slightly hesitantly.

"Hi!" I nodded back, including the girl in my greeting. She smiled and looked over my shoulder at the circle where the seventy Dawn Patrollers were praying.

"What are you all doing?" asked the guy. He seemed genuinely bewildered. "We saw you from over there," he pointed to grass-topped dunes rising from the beach, "and wondered what's up with the circle and the cross."

I was amazed that they had been intrigued by what we were doing and excited by the fact that they also had the courage to come over and ask about it.

I stepped out of the circle and explained that we were Christians who had come to Newquay to pray for the town, to help where we could and to talk about Jesus with anyone who was interested.

They both listened intently and nodded as I spoke. There was a pause as I finished. I smiled, wondering if anything I had said would send them running back to the dunes.

"That sounds good, man," said the guy after a moment. "It's about time some people did something good in this town," he continued

"There's some bad stuff here," the girl added. "The tourists just see one side but once you've been here a while, you find out that Newquay is a dark place."

My brow furrowed but I nodded as if I understood.

"Thanks anyway, man," the guy said, offering me his hand to shake. "All the best with what you're trying to do, and that." Then, over his shoulder: "Respect!" he called back to me, before the pair of them strolled off, across the sand towards the hoards of sunbathers.

I watched them go as Dawn Patrollers continued to pray. Inside me I sensed a prompting to run after them. I tried to ignore it and searched my mind for an excuse not to do it.

The couple gradually looked smaller as the distance between us increased.

The feeling didn't go away. They would soon disappear from my sight. If I was going to go after them I would need to decide quickly.

Oh, bum! I thought to myself as I broke out of the circle and, without explanation to anyone, I ran across the sand. As I approached from behind them I began to wonder what I was going to say. Would impulses like that begin to take over my life now I'd given in once? I didn't have time for that thought to bother me though because by now I was right behind them and I'd need to say something quickly if I wasn't going to look like a weirdo.

"Hi. . ." I offered at their backs. As they turned around I pulled the most disarming smile I could manage and began to explain, very quickly, that I had been really impressed that they had asked me about the gathering and that perhaps there was more to talk about.

"Sure," said the guy, much to my profound amazement and relief. "Your friends are still praying, right?" he asked, pointing back along the beach towards the circle of Dawn Patrollers.

I nodded.

"Do you really think it makes a difference?" the girl asked.

"Prayer changes things," I said. And I meant it. The events of that week had convinced me that prayer was the only thing that could lead to an impact on people's lives or, for that matter, the darkness that existed under the surface in Newquay.

"Maybe you're right," she replied. "It doesn't matter to me, I'm out of here anyway. I'm going to India to live with a guru."

I wasn't sure about how to reply so I just listened while she proceeded to tell me about what she was going to be doing. As she spoke I prayed silently. I didn't know what to ask God but I wanted him to be involved in what was going on so I simply offered that desire to him and trusted that he would take my motivation and do something cool with it.

I asked why she had decided to go and, as she spoke animatedly about how dead-end and generally rubbish her life in England was, our mutual trust in the conversation seemed to deepen.

An exchange of information became due and they asked me about my beliefs. I explained that I believed God had revealed himself in Jesus Christ and that in doing so he'd provided tangible hope of transformation for our lives that had immediate and eternal significance. It was a heavy subject but I could sense that God's Spirit was helping me to say things lightly – not guiding the words exactly but he gave the whole thing integrity and a deep significance.

The couple listened respectfully and asked probing questions about what my understanding was based upon. They made it clear that although the theme of transformation that I had touched on was something that interested both of them, they shared a deep-seated distrust of institutional religion and for that reason, couldn't seriously consider Christianity for themselves at that stage in their lives.

As the conversation drew to a natural close it was obvious that all three of us would take something deep away. I was pleased that I hadn't ignored the urge to run after them.

I turned back towards the Dawn Patrollers to see that the circle had mutated into clusters of people chatting around a large bundle of lads mucking around and wrestling. The prayers were clearly finished.

As I moved across the sand towards them, I looked out to sea. The waves were dotted with surfers, as on the day I arrived, when I'd been full of apprehension about what the week might hold. I stopped for a moment. The sun sparkled on the water like golden freckles.

The conversation with the dreadlocked couple

lingered in my mind. I turned back to look at the crowds of sunbathing clubbers covering the sand and the feeling I had begun to recognise before speaking to the couple surfaced again – this time very clearly. It was accompanied by a sense of excitement. As I looked at the sunbathing clubbers, I was looking at the future.

God had always been working in Newquay and always would be. The seventy of us taking part in Dawn Patrol had joined in for a week and been changed in the process and there was no looking back – no chance of being un-transformed. Not for me, or any of the Dawn Patrollers, or anyone whose life God had used us to touch. But there was more to do. More than I could begin to imagine.

I knew what the feeling inside me was. God was inviting me to come back to Newquay the following summer. Even as I realised what he was asking, I knew what my answer would be.

PART 2

The Apprentice Samaritan

The drunk keeled slowly to one side and slumped on the pavement. I maintained my pace and continued down the high street.

A tiny part of me – a part stuffed in a crevice somewhere in my conscience – protested that I should have stopped to check that the guy was OK. Perhaps done something to help him?

I tried to dismiss the situation with cool rationale: someone else had probably stopped to help. And anyway, he was only drunk – it was probably best to leave him alone to sleep it off.

I felt uncomfortable though. Should I have helped immediately while I had the chance? What was the point of coming to Newquay on a second summer of mission – a mission in which I would be leading a small team – if my reaction to a glaringly obvious need was to walk by without pausing? I decided to try and learn from the incident and do things differently in the future.

In the meantime I continued on my way down the busy high street, which looked exactly as it had done the previous summer – except busier. In fact, the place was rammed. It seemed as if everyone who had visited the year before had gone home and told all their mates and they'd all decided to give Newquay a go.

I felt unexpectedly overwhelmed. I'd had a year to prepare but there were so many people. I began to wonder, as I had the year before, how we would know who to speak to and how we would be bold with our message and sensitive to people's circumstances at the same time.

As I wove in and out of the holidaymakers jamming the high street like reeds packed along the edge of a lake, I began to pray silently inside myself that God would give me courage and a simple trust that he had everything under control.

By the end of the afternoon almost one hundred Dawn Patrollers would have arrived in town. I knew that we would be involved in some crazy stuff. I also knew that I didn't have much of an idea about how to do the job I had agreed to take on.

I would be leading the clubbing team. At that moment I couldn't have felt less up to the task. We would be going into the town's bars and among the thousands of clubbers, to serve, to listen – to try to demonstrate God's love with our words and deeds.

My only real experience of leadership, however,

had been as a corporal in the army cadets when I was sixteen. I doubted whether this would be the sort of experience I'd be able to call on in New-quay. There wouldn't be too much demand for building bivouacs or cleaning rifles. . .

I wondered what sort of job I'd make of pulling people together. Or helping everyone to give their best. Or guiding the team into doing something worthwhile. . . If God didn't help me, the whole thing would be going pear-shaped pretty quickly.

I was going to need a serious injection of every-thing God could possibly provide: wisdom, guid-ance, support, protection and all-round help. But that was fine. I told myself to think about the pre-vious year's mission and how God had gently and faithfully come up with the goods. He had led me through the challenges of that week by making his presence obvious and his ability unquestionable.

I wasn't up to leading a team or sharing my faith with anyone, but God was. Nevertheless, a part of me still wondered if I was entirely prepared to believe that. The fact was that the week ahead would be where trust in God would have to become a reality.

The high street was crammed with young people. They scurried about, bursting with energy, eager eyes dancing all over each other. It was like watching masses of puppies impatient for someone to take them home and play with them and love them. I was having trouble imagining how a bunch of young Christians could make any kind of impact. There were just so many people.

"What do you want us to do here Lord?" I prayed.

I was serious.

I continued praying as I walked through the town, past the sprawling Central pub and down the slip road that dropped in a steep curve to the little harbour.

On the broad wall of the harbour I found a bench and plonked myself down among the flapping, squawking gulls and the tourists who ambled aimlessly, stuffing large, dribbly ice creams into their mouths. In the water below, a bulky fishing boat, its deck converted to take benches for day trippers instead of nets, was chugging towards the harbour entrance, it's chubby cargo decked out in bright waterproofs and be-dangled with camcorders.

I let my concerns about the week ahead and my prayers for help roll around inside my head. Gradually, as I sat among the bustle, a deep stillness filled me and I sensed God's whisper – devoid of words but announcing unmistakably, "Don't be afraid. Concentrate on me."

The awareness that God has gigantic ability to plan things down to infinitesimal details (most of which we are often too busy to spot) grew and sparkled in my mind like bright rays of light prodding through the leaves of a tree. God had brought me and each of the other Dawn Patrollers to Newquay to speak to particular people. We would meet them without worrying about it. Each of us would say things that God could use even if we only managed to jabber a few fumbled sentences.

Feeling a whole lot more peaceful about what the week might have in store, I jumped up and headed down from the harbour across Towan beach towards the flat that would be the home I'd be sharing with my wife and our baby daughter for the week.

~

Above Towan beach there is a large grassy area affectionately known as the killer-court (apparently they used to hang criminals there centuries back). My walk home took me across the middle of it.

Unusually it was not particularly busy at that moment. The crazy-golf course, which occupies one corner, was playing host to an elderly couple and a young seagull whose head was lost in a flurry of fish and chip papers.

As I crossed the killer-court, feeling encouraged by my experience on the harbour wall, I happened to look across the golf course towards the United Reformed church which flanks it. As I did so, a man came stumbling around the corner. I recognised him instantly. It was the drunk guy that I'd seen pass out on the high street twenty minutes before.

Helping him along (or rather supporting him almost entirely) was a woman in her thirties, who didn't look particularly strong. The woman's two young children were also helping.

Shocked, I stopped dead in my tracks.

As I watched the scene unfolding, I wondered briefly if the guy was her husband whom she'd come to drag home. It was soon obvious that he wasn't and that she had no reason to help him at all. In fact, if anyone had a good reason *not* to help a comatose drunk who probably stank of urine and vomit, it was a woman out with her kids. How did she know that he wouldn't abuse her or her children in some way? I guessed she didn't. But nevertheless, there they were, the three of them, helping him away from the high street to a quiet bench where he wouldn't be trampled or kicked and where he could gather himself with at least a bit of dignity.

The little family's actions boomed across the killer-court at me like a clap of thunder. What they were doing, with only me to observe (the young seagull and the golfers were preoccupied), spoke more powerfully than vast volumes of words.

It was like watching a real-life version of Jesus' Good Samaritan parable. I realised that in the real-life version of the story that I was witnessing, I had already given myself the part of the priest who walked past the injured man without stopping to help.

In those few moments a profoundly simple lesson was branded onto me: If I saw someone in need I *could* help. There was no adequate excuse for walking away – not one worthy reason for me to leave the job to someone else.

In the actions of the woman and her children, God was speaking about what to do that week. In the middle of everything that would come, my team and I would be on the look out for people who needed obvious help. We wouldn't hang around trying to think of reasons to do nothing – we would get stuck right in.

I couldn't have known how quickly I would be putting my new resolution to the test.

The Basement

My eight-month-old daughter was trapped in a beanbag.

Minutes after the experience on the killer-court, I walked through the door of the tiny, top-floor flat that was our home for the week to find Rachel, my wife, spooning food into our daughter's mouth. With no high chair available, Rachel had ingeniously plonked Hannah into the centre of a large beanbag from which she could not escape. It was a funny sight.

I gave them both a kiss, flopped down on the sofa and gazed at the sea, which was framed by the room's disproportionately large window. The little living room was cosy in spite of the expanse of glass. Books and videos lined a stack of shelves, a small TV sat in a corner and a soft rug filled the floor.

The flat belonged to a woman called Maggie who had given it up for the week to allow Rachel and Hannah to come to Newquay with me. Her generosity left me wondering how quickly I would move out of my home for a week so that a young family could use it (especially when one member was fond of mashed banana but hadn't really mastered the art of keeping it all in her mouth).

I was pleased that the girls were going to be with me but getting and keeping a balance between my responsibilities to them and the mission team would be a heavy challenge.

I had heard about pastors who were so busy doing "God's" work that they spent no time with their families and ended up with their marriages falling apart. As far as I could see, being a good husband and father was *part* of God's work and that meant making time to be with my family.

For me, the week would be mostly night shifts and, I suspected, a good few adrenaline highs. For Rachel, on the other hand, the reality would be the daily routine of childcare. Out marriage would need God's support and both of us would be needing plenty of grace. It would be important that Rachel knew she and Hannah were right at the top of my priorities.

I made us some lunch and Rachel and I ate together on the sofa and enjoyed watching Hannah, released from the beanbag, crawling around, discovering her new environment. For her everything was exciting. There was nothing that wasn't worth picking up and sucking.

I wanted to have a similar approach to the week ahead. Not shoving everything into my dribbly mouth, but I wanted to explore and be excited by everything. I was eager to get stuck in, whatever the circumstances.

An hour later I was standing in the United Reformed church (URC) looking at my team – the "clubbers" team – and wondering what on earth God might have been thinking of when he brought them to Newquay. The excitement I had resolved to have, whistled out of me like air escaping from a punctured tyre.

We had formed a rough circle in a corner of the church. The building was hot and packed with Dawn Patrollers finding their teams, shifting bags and making a hundred noisy introductions.

I looked around at my team – from one to the next. I wasn't quite sure what I *was* expecting but it wasn't the group shaking hands with each other and grinning at me at that moment. They were an equal mix of girls and lads ranging in age from eighteen to thirty and were, I don't think it's unkind to say, completely unglamorous (I include myself in that remark!)

Being unglamorous was obviously fine – we weren't in Newquay to impress anyone with our slick styles. However, in my pre-mission imaginings, I had conjured up a picture of a group who at least *looked* familiar with club culture. Barring two or three, not many of the group fitted my picture.

In fact, a couple of them looked to me as if they hadn't been to a town centre after 5pm let alone visited a bar or a nightclub! I wondered if they would cope, let alone be any use.

But it was too late for worrying about who should be on the team. We were all there and that was that. We'd have to get on with it. If some didn't know anything about clubbing, they soon would! And if God had put the team together, then I'd have to trust him and get on with leading it! Perhaps *I* would be surprised? Perhaps, I told myself, I was being too quick to judge by appearance. I would soon find out. . .

"*Clubbing* team?" A young woman with an American accent poked her head into our circle. Everyone looked at me.

"Er, yes!" I raised my eyebrows and nodded.

"Hi!" She waved a hand around the group by way of greeting.

"I'm Laura," she continued. "If you could grab your bags and follow me, I'll show you where you'll be staying for the week!" She sounded very positive about everything. I imagined that the team's accommodation would be equally sunny.

As it turned out, five minutes later, the sleeping quarters were not quite as bright as Laura's cheery tones.

121

We found ourselves standing on a chipped lino floor in a dim, church hall basement. A subtle dampness hovered around the edges of the room. Laura pointed out the kitchen area and some ropy shower cubicles. I hadn't told the team that I would, unfortunately, not be staying with them but would have the hardship of having to sleep in a real bed in a comfortable flat. Looking around at their slightly concerned faces, I thought it might be best to leave the announcement until a better time. . .

We were in the basement, Laura explained, *because we would no doubt be sleeping in the day a fair bit and wouldn't want to be disturbed by the sunshine.* . . I suppose she had a point, in a roundabout way.

Although I was (extremely) pleased to be sleeping in a bed in a cosy flat rather than on the cold, hard basement floor of a church hall, I was a bit worried that I might not bond properly with the team. Didn't real leaders muck in with the troops, so to speak? Didn't leaders who earned respect and achieved worthwhile things experience the same hardships as those they led?

As the guys began to spread out their roll mats and sleeping bags, I remembered that Jesus had said something about leaders serving those they led. I wondered if that meant I should give a different team member a chance to sleep in the flat each night while I slept in the basement. . . I wasn't sure Rachel would be all that impressed with that idea. I'd just have to make sure that I was around as much as possible. The leadership thing was already getting a bit tricky and we hadn't even started.

Laura left us alone to get settled in. We chatted as the guys spread out their gear. The only comments about the accommodation were made in joke form but for the most part, the team just got on with getting to know each other. Everyone seemed pleased to be in Newquay and eager to get started on whatever it was we were going to be doing. Their keenness put some air back in my metaphorical tyre.

Eventually the fifteen of us found ourselves sitting and talking in the rough circle that had naturally formed earlier in the URC and which would form again and again throughout the week.

Everyone appeared enthusiastic but didn't seem naturally outgoing – and I sensed varying degrees of apprehension which reminded me, in a small way, of myself the previous summer (except that no one appeared to be having an obvious doubt-and-fear-faith-crisis). I wondered how I would deal with any personal faith traumas if they came up. Although I felt completely unqualified for dealing with the possibility of a team member struggling with what we would be doing, I supposed that in a bizarre way, my struggles the previous summer put me in a good position to offer some guidance. I would have to cross that bridge if and when I came to it.

Before I left the basement, I told my team that we would be prayer-walking the town late that night. My plan was for us to wait until it was pub-chucking-out time so that we could plunge right in at the deep end and experience the full impact of Saturday night on the streets of Newquay. That way, I figured, everyone would know straight away what kind of week we were in for.

I headed up the rough, wooden stairs to the street. Perhaps I was beginning to feel what being a "leader" meant. I knew what the team might experience that night and I wondered if, for some of them, it might all be a bit too much. There was a strong possibility that the team would have shrunk by the following afternoon.

Techno-heads

I could hear the music as I walked up the steps to the front door of the building that contained our flat.

I looked up to find that the windows of the flat next to ours, on the second floor, were wide open. Out of them rolled a chaotic, bass-heavy dance track. Usually I wouldn't have minded – I like dance music – but if it was that loud out on the street, I could only imagine what it would be like inside the tiny flat where I had assumed Rachel and Hannah would be able to spend calm, quiet evenings chilling out with books and games and a bit of TV.

When I stepped through the doorway I found that things were as bad as I'd begun to imagine. Rachel was upset but seemed to be holding things together better than I would have done in the circumstances. She was bravely attempting to watch TV in spite of the fact that the living room was almost alive with the sound of next door's music. I immediately felt angry.

Amazingly, Hannah was curled up asleep in her little travel cot in the bedroom, oblivious to the thump-thump invading from the other side of the wall.

"I'm going round!" I announced, impetuously.

I felt it was my manly duty to deal with the problem and bring relief to my distressed wife.

"No!" Rachel pulled the rug out from beneath my gallant feet. "We don't want to mess things up for Maggie."

Rachel had a point of course. I didn't want Maggie – the owner of our flat – to return to a neighbour-from-hell situation and a stack of hate mail. On the other hand, perhaps I would be doing her a favour if I went round and told the guy that all his neighbours would be happy to club together for a pair of headphones or even pay for him to go to a nightclub like everyone else!

But Rachel was insistent: I wasn't to go round. He'd probably turn it off in a minute when he went out, she offered hopefully; and anyway, he was a big, mean-looking guy.

I (reluctantly) gave in and we sat on the sofa together pretending that we could hear what was being said on the TV. The tunes rolled mercilessly on and on and, it seemed, got even louder.

After a while it became obvious that Mr Mean next door wasn't going out any time soon. I began to wonder, in a nightmarish way, if he'd fallen into a drug-induced coma with the CD stuck on repeat – that perhaps there would be no end to the noise, just a night of Rachel and I lying in bed, staring at the ceiling and going slowly insane. The basement where the team would be spending the night began to seem strangely appealing. . .

After what seemed like a very long time of pretending to be patient and feeling increasingly frustrated, angry and helpless, I leapt to my feet.

We had to do something.

Or rather, *something* had to happen. The situation was ridiculous. I had planned to go out prayer-walking with my team that evening. But that would mean leaving Rachel and Hannah alone with a techno-soundtrack. Putting my wife through an evening of torture had not been in my plan.

If I was going to focus and lead the team well that night and throughout the week, I needed to know that Rachel and Hannah were safe, calm and comfortable. As things stood at that moment, I was going to be spending the evening worrying and trying to find us alternative accommodation.

I couldn't believe that would be necessary though. I had gone to Newquay to share my faith because I believed in a God who is real, present and capable of prompt, tangible help. I claimed to believe in a God who was bothered about even the tiniest detail and for whom no task was too large.

God knew as well as we did that the music thumping into our heads from next door was a real and immediate problem which, given that it was Maggie's home and not our own, we were not really in a position to sort out via the usual channels.

Basically we needed a miracle. God knew it as well as we did but we needed to ask him.

I was a little hesitant at first to mention this to Rachel. I chewed it over while standing with my hands on my hips in the centre of the gently vibrating living room.

I was hesitant because I didn't want us to agree to pray only for nothing to happen. At the start of a week that was going to require a mountain of faith, I didn't want to risk a serious dent in our stockpile.

Rachel stared at me from the sofa. It wasn't until she put her hands on her head in despair that I sat down beside her and took hold of her knee as I (loudly) made my suggestion:

"Let's pray about this. . ."

Rachel nodded and closed her eyes. She had obviously reached the same conclusion as me about the needing-a-miracle thing.

I took a deep breath and tried to focus my full attention on God. It wasn't easy. I am easily distracted at the best of times and this was certainly not the best of times. But I was desperate. We needed help. Soon.

I began to explain carefully to God that we had come to Newquay because of him – because we had felt that was where *he* wanted us. I realised that he knew all of that already but I wanted him to know that I knew it too. . .

"If we're going to do this week properly, it's going to be hard work," I continued (along with the music), "and Rachel and Hannah are going to need to be peaceful in the flat." Rachel squeezed my hand. "And we're all going to need good sleep and the music next door is just way too loud. Please could you, in some way, get the guy to turn it down and keep it down. . ."

As I said that line something happened that made Rachel and me sit up straight.

Large grins formed on our faces.

The music was beginning to fade.

I pressed on with the end of the prayer slowly, trying not to break into a laugh of utter disbelief.

The music continued to fade to a dim thud and as I finished speaking it was gone. Completely.

Rachel and I sat in silence, our mouths open, our eyes popping, as we gawked, whopping, huge smiles. We waited for the music to kick back on again at any second.

It didn't.

Nothing. Absolutely nothing.

We waited five minutes, laughing quiet, disbelieving laughs.

Ten minutes passed and not a peep.

God had just blown both our minds and it was not to be the last time that week either.

Dead Man Walking

I ducked to avoid a life-sized inflatable rubber doll that had just been punched out of the hands of the guy I was passing. His mates jeered and laughed as he scrabbled around trying to snatch her up again. Girls and lads heading up and down the high street around us joined in with lairy shouts and comments.

It was almost midnight as I led my team on our first prayer walk. All of us were decked out in red hoodies emblazoned with the Dawn Patrol logo. I stuffed my hands into the large front pocket of mine. Our movement was slow as we pushed our way through the hoards of clubbers moving drunkenly from the pubs and bars to an assortment of kebab shops, chippys and nightclubs.

We were strung out in threes and fours and were supposed to be praying. Things around us were so full-on, however, that any kind of focused prayer was all but impossible unless we'd been wearing blindfolds and earplugs. We weren't.

If we were failing in the first goal, we were more than successful in my second, namely that the team get a decent idea of night life in Newquay. The alcohol-fuelled carnival surrounding us was a prime example of what to expect in the week ahead.

We began to head out of the town centre, past the harbour slip road and along to the supermarket plonked on a rise above it. I suggested that we scatter ourselves around the steps that led up to the supermarket to spend five minutes in silent prayer, asking God to work in the lives of the hundreds of people we had just walked among. Our prayers would make a difference.

As I began to pray silently, I looked around at the team and noticed how odd we must have looked (to anyone who might have been sober) walking along together, all dressed in the same red tops. It made me smile. Being dressed in identical yellow t-shirts had really bothered me the previous summer. I was surprised to realise that my feelings had changed to the point where I thought it was great that we stood out. The red made us look a bit like a bunch of lifeguards which, in a curious way, I suppose we were.

On the road below us couples and small groups passed noisily on their way to Fistral beach with bottles of wine and odd pieces of rubbish to use as firewood.

The team seemed to take seriously my suggested task of praying, but as the five minutes quickly elapsed, I began to realise that I didn't have much of an idea about what to do next. Barring God, there was no one around for me to grab a bit of advice from.

Being the team leader suddenly felt like a very lonely job. It was up to me to appear confident and make a coherent decision about where we were to go. It was tempting to call it a night and return to the calm safety of the basement.

I stood up and stretched. Above us the inky sky was scattered with stars. It was a great night. It would have been a nice evening for a walk along the beach with Rachel. I pushed that thought out of my mind. I was there to lead a mission and the guys were beginning to stand and look to me for directions. I had to think quickly.

"Let's head towards Fistral," I announced.

Only I knew how lame this suggestion was – that it seemed to me to come more from desperation than inspiration – but it was the best I could do. I would find out shortly that in spite of my feelings, the suggestion had indeed been inspired.

"That way we will have prayer-walked from one end of the town to the other and got our heads around the place. . ." I supposed there was a rough logic in my thinking.

Although they weren't enthusiastic, the team received my suggestion as if it were as good as any other and slowly, almost lethargically, we made our way down onto the street.

Hoods were pulled up over heads and hands were stuffed heavily in pockets. It was a chilly night. I wondered if there was a slight frustration brewing that we weren't getting stuck into something more specific – something *real*, whatever that might be.

I didn't need to worry. Before long a very real test was facing us.

I could make it out 100 metres before we reached it – a dark, person-sized heap blocking the pavement on a corner up ahead. A couple of teenagers were standing a few feet to one side eating chips.

We sped up, concerned to discover what was going on.

"Is he dead?" one of the teenagers asked with a bizarre degree of enthusiasm.

I bent over, along with Paul and Nick, two of my team, and looked carefully at the man's face. He wasn't dead. Drunk and unconscious yes, but not dead – not quite.

His body was wrapped in a scruffy black overcoat. He wore heavy army boots, had long, grey-blond hair and high, prominent cheekbones that lent his face a striking look. In the dim light provided by the street lamp he appeared to be in his late thirties. He stank of booze.

"Is he dead?" asked the guy with the chips again.

"Arghhh!" A girl who had just arrived with a group of friends screamed. "Someone's dead on the pavement!" she added unhelpfully.

I stood up and put them straight.

"He's not dead – just drunk."

"Leave 'im then. What're you doing messin' about with 'im?" yelled one of the girl's companions.

"Let 'im sleep it off," added another.

I looked around at my team. They looked back at me. Paul and Nick continued to kneel beside the unconscious guy, trying to get some sort of response from him.

I knew that we had to help. I wasn't sure how, but we could work out the details as we went along. Whatever, we definitely weren't leaving him to sleep it off – I'd done that once already that day and had resolved never to do it again.

More party-people were arriving from the direction of the town centre. My team was waiting to hear what the plan was. I needed to act quickly.

Billions of Naked Christians?

"Cheers for getting me off the street! Who knows what might have happened if you'd left me there?" Tom, the drunk guy whom Paul, Nick and I had helped the previous night was sitting opposite us wearing a large grin and had just raised a pint of lager in an over-dramatic gesture of salute.

We were sitting in The Vic – a proper old-rockers pub tucked away deceptively in an alley. A Guns-n-Roses anthem rumbled across the bare floorboards, giving a natural feel to the excess of leather, chains and long black hair worn by those around us.

Tom's ruddy face and intelligent eyes retained an almost permanent smile as he chatted away. When we had found him the night before, the dim street lamps had distorted his features, making him look far older than his twenty-one years. He spoke well and had an unusual confidence that hinted at an expensive education.

~

After we had stopped to help him, Paul, Nick and I had managed to raise Tom into consciousness and help him to a near-by bench. He'd been incoherent at first but after half an hour he'd sobered up enough to ask us what had made us stop and help him.

The three of us had pieced together an answer based around the fact that we were Christians. He'd looked at us with interest and surprise. We'd reassured him that we hadn't helped him with some kind of an ulterior motive in mind. We'd come to Newquay to make God's love real somehow, not to preach at people who couldn't get away.

A thoughtful conversation about God had evolved until eventually we decided unanimously that it was officially freezing. I had asked Tom if we could meet him the following night to carry on the conversation.

The Vic had been his suggestion but I'd reckoned the chances of him remembering were about zero. It was with surprise, therefore, that we found ourselves sitting around a table in a pub full of rockers, listening to heavy metal and talking about Jesus.

Tom was a bright guy. He asked tough, perceptive questions and listened carefully to how we answered him about our faith in God.

As we talked, he leapt up at regular intervals to visit the bar for more pints. He was drinking quickly, clearly wanting to make the most of his evening and to down as many pints as possible.

As time sped by, Tom gave away parts of his story – a story that was well masked by the ragged coat, army boots and living (without too much washing) in a tent.

His parents were wealthy racehorse breeders. They had sent him to a famous public boarding school and they expected big things from him. Fed up with all these expectations, he had headed to Cornwall, wanting to find space to think things through. He hadn't been in touch with his parents for weeks.

I asked him if he intended to let them know at some point that he was still alive.

"Probably. . ." He took a swig of lager. "But not tonight! They're a couple of losers," he added with a laugh, before adding something that surprised me.

"I've been thinking about you three stopping to help me last night and I don't think it was a coincidence."

I raised my eyebrows, grinned to show him that I agreed, and nodded him on.

He explained that he believed a "benevolent force of some kind" was protecting him and suggested that was what had made us help him. For a moment I suspected that he was winding us up. I looked him carefully in the eyes. He meant it. He was serious.

I explained, as well as I could, that I believed this "benevolent force" had a name: Jesus. I went on to say that it was because of our relationships with Jesus that the three of us had bothered to stop and help.

He rocked his head from side to side, apparently digesting the idea.

"Perhaps you're right!" he announced with a slight air of arrogance. "The thing is. . ." he paused for a moment and looked at us each in turn before continuing, "if God is going to help me whenever I'm in trouble, why do I need a relationship with him?"

He took several gulps of lager, draining the glass.

"I mean, what's the point?" he went on. "It's all

the same in the end isn't it? God will help if he wants to and if he doesn't feel like it, he won't. You three should just relax and party like everyone else." He swept his arm around the increasingly busy pub clutching the empty pint glass as if to give emphasis to his theory.

It was difficult to reply to what he had said. I made an effort but sensed a change in the atmosphere. I tried to tell him that it wasn't simply about whether or not God would help you out when you needed him to but it was about realising that the very purpose of our existence is to have a relationship with God. But Tom seemed to have lost interest both in the conversation, and in us. The music had been turned up and a group of attractive girls was standing beside our table. Tom's mind had moved on to other things.

The conversation began to go in large circles, regularly interrupted by Tom's visits to the bar. I noticed also that he was staying away from our table for longer each time and coming back with questions or arguments about God that were less coherent and accompanied by more laughter. I felt that perhaps it was time to wish him a good night, leave him to it and go and find the rest of my team.

I leant close to Paul and yelled my thoughts in his ear. He nodded and yelled back that, after three hours of God-talk, he was all out of spiritual energy.

At that moment Tom returned from the bar with two shot glasses of vodka. He tilted his head back and necked them both in quick succession, following them with a question that reassured me that it was indeed time to leave:

"If we are all born naked, right. . ."

I could tell from the smug expression hanging behind his drunken grin, that he thought he had a real killer of a question – something that would leave us stumped and helpless.

". . .then Christians are upsetting God by wearing clothes aren't they? You're sinning because you're doing something that God never wanted you to do." He delivered what he thought was the final blow with the kind of misplaced confidence only achieved by drinking far too much alcohol.

I looked at Paul and Nick. Nick had a furrowed brow. I could almost see the cogs turning – searching for a suitable reply. Paul, on the other hand, was shaking his head and wearing a dismayed grin that described what I was feeling. It was time to leave.

"So by wearing clothes, Christians are showing that they're all hypocrites!" Tom concluded, pronouncing the words with the finality of a judge who had just passed sentence.

With an attempt at some kind of humorous answer, we stood up, thanking Tom for a good conversation, and told him that we had to go. He climbed gingerly to his feet with loud goodbyes and then, with drunken, back-slapping hugs, wished us all the best and offered us his mobile number.

As Paul, Nick and I pushed between two enormous bouncers out into the Newquay night, I felt drained. I was tempted to feel defeated as well.

We weren't quite leaving with our tails between our legs but we didn't exactly have an amazing story of radical conversion to tell either. Nevertheless, somewhere deep down I knew I was wrong to have wanted another dramatic miracle. It wasn't up to us to convince people about God – that was his specialist area. Our job was to help where we saw a need and speak up when the opportunity arose. We had done both, comprehensively.

As we set off to find the rest of the team, I reminded myself that I would have to forget about looking for "results" during the mission. If I was going to see people as fellow human beings instead of targets for evangelism, I needed to start trusting my efforts to God and relax my own grip on things.

Recreational Enlightenment?

I sat on a bar stool, praying silently that God would help two girls from my team – Sarah and Louise – to know what to say to the two lads with whom they had just begun a conversation.

I'd found them in the bar twenty minutes after leaving The Vic. As I'd pulled up a stool, I overheard Sarah asking one of the lads:

"If it was possible to have a personal relationship with God, would you be interested?"

From what I could see; the lads were definitely interested in something. Whether it was God would remain to be seen.

In the short time I had spent with them that week, I had realised that Sarah and Louise were a potent combination. Sarah was bright with a gentle charisma. I'd noticed that, whenever she spoke, people stopped to listen. Louise, a shrewd fashion student, had a streetwise air that meant people were intrigued to find out she was a Christian and wanted to find out more. I could see from the lads' expressions and body language that everything about these two girls was pushing them to reassess their ideas about what being a Christian might involve.

There was always the risk that the girls' bold approach could be misinterpreted and that the lads would be thinking it was their lucky night. If that was the case, the girls would no doubt soon put them straight. They wanted to share their faith, not get phone numbers, and they weren't going to be distracted. I was impressed with their calm but dedicated approach and wondered what God might do with it.

I continued to pray for the conversation but decided to leave the girls to it for a few minutes. I made my way to the door of the busy bar, dodging around an animated group as they tumbled indoors from the street.

Outside, the street was calmer. The bar was called On the Rocks, situated at the top of the cliffs looking out over Towan beach. It was away from the main high street and was slightly quieter than many of the town's bars, although the back-end of the gigantic Walkabout club was only a few metres away and, by the sound of it, already getting busy.

Taking a lung-full of bracing, night-time sea air, I walked across to the railings that bordered the road at the cliff edge. Above me, against the black cloth of the sky, several seagulls hung on the breeze, screeching, their white undersides illuminated by the glow from the streetlamps.

A group of rowdy partygoers passed behind me as I leant over the railings and gazed down at the beach below. I was surprised to see that although the tide had swamped most of the sand and was licking eagerly at the slim crescent left exposed, there was nevertheless a fair crowd of young people dancing, drinking and running naked into the sea.

I had only just begun to watch what was taking place at the edge of the cold, dark water for a moment when I felt a tap on the arm.

I turned my head to find an animated, red-haired guy aged around nineteen standing beside me. I looked him up and down as he offered a friendly greeting.

"Alright mate!" he chirped. "Have you got any Es for sale at all?"

I grinned, several possibilities suggesting themselves simultaneously in my mind, and then turned to face him properly before opting for my answer.

"You've asked the wrong bloke, mate," I said, opening my arms slightly and spreading the upturned palms of my hands in a gesture of frank honesty.

The pally eagerness that had been written across his face was replaced by an edge of slight concern.

He stepped back half a pace as the question left his lips. "You're not undercover police are you?"

"No!" I shook my head with amusement. "Why? Do I look like one?"

"Not really; that's why I asked you about the Es." He smiled, I guessed more from relief than friendliness.

"I'm a Christian," I ventured by way of further explanation.

In the years I had spent clubbing, I'd been asked for drugs countless times but never once used the words I had just uttered as an explanation for not having any. Being on the mission meant that my faith was in the forefront of my mind though so, out of curiosity, I'd thought I might as well announce it and see where it took the conversation.

"Oh!" the guy exclaimed with a mixture of politeness, slight embarrassment at what he had asked me, and a sudden, urgent eagerness to get away. He didn't disappear immediately however, but stood, looking at me quizzically, unsure about how to disentangle himself without offence.

I prayed a quick, silent prayer, asking God to show me what, if anything, to say and to use the brief encounter to speak to him.

It was the other guy's turn to speak.

"I'm actually a Buddhist," he announced.

"Really?" I raised both eyebrows in genuine surprise. "So what's with trying to score Es?"

He shrugged.

"Aren't you supposed to be searching for enlightenment?" I asked, genuinely puzzled.

He smiled, acknowledging my point, and made himself a concession.

"Yeah, well, I'm not a full-on Buddhist but I try not to cause harm to anyone. And I *do* meditate!"

"Oh!" Wanting to appear open to his approach, I opened my eyes a little wider than usual and pushed my lower lip against the top one, forcing them to protrude slightly.

"I did look at Christianity for a bit," he went on, shifting from one foot to the other. "It says some good things. But I'm young, I mean I'm younger than you – no offence – and I've got my whole life to think about religion and God. Right now, to be honest, I just want to have a good time. . . 'Know what I mean?"

He rolled his shoulders and sniffed.

"I know what you mean," I said in a tone that suggested I didn't particularly agree with his logic. What he had said reminded me of the conversation I'd finished having with Tom less than an hour before. It seemed that in the minds of these two young guys, the concept of knowing God was utterly incompatible with living life to the full. In their minds the two were diametrically opposed lifestyles.

"Exactly!" He snatched at my words as if we were now on a wave-length of understanding that would allow him to continue his quest for ecstasy satisfied that, thankfully, there was no need to re-think any part of his life at all. I guessed that he was set on his goal of a night spent feeling like nothing in the world mattered, or ever would.

The problem, which I knew well from my own crashing experiences, was that when the night was over, the come-down swept into your mind like a grey day, replacing the illusions of euphoria with bleak, glacial emptiness.

There was also the risk, when you were buying drugs from total strangers – as my fidgety new acquaintance was intending to do – that you were going to end up taking horse tranquillisers or something cut with bleach that could put you in a morgue before the music had stopped the next morning.

A thought came into my mind which I turned into a question.

"When you were looking at Christianity," I asked, "did you ever hear any of the things that

Jesus said?" I kept the tone light and interested. I didn't want him to assume I had a long, heavy conversation in mind.

He took a deep breath, which I read as impatience.

"Look, sorry mate," I offered, wanting him to feel he could leave whenever. "If you need to get going, that's cool. I was just interested – that's all."

"No, it's fine." He sounded genuine. "I did, yeah. I can't really remember much of it though. I know he said some good things. . ."

"There was something Jesus said that I thought you should hear," I said. A verse from the Bible had swum into my mind and I wanted to offer it to this guy to chew over.

"Yeah?" He seemed keen enough to hear it.

"Yeah." I tried to keep my voice animated. "Jesus said I am the way, the truth and the life. He didn't say the way for olds who've finished partying." The guy was listening intently. "He said that there is real truth out there and that it's *him*. And that real life, I mean *real* life – if you want to find it – is in him."

There was a moment of silence. We stared at each other for a split second. And then it was his turn to push his bottom lip up and out and nod his head slowly.

148

"Thanks for that," he offered in a flat tone that left me guessing what was going through his mind.

"I'm James, by the way." He held out a hand enthusiastically.

"I'm Michael – and it was good to meet you," I told him, shaking his hand. "I can't say I hope you find any drugs," I smiled. "But have a good night, whatever."

He thanked me and, somewhat ironically, told me to "take care", before disappearing down the alley along the side of the Walkabout club.

I turned back towards the sea and prayed silently that God would work in James' heart and pump some life into the words of Jesus that I had introduced to him.

As I looked down across the growing crowd on the beach, some of the feelings of discouragement began to surface just as I'd experienced after chatting to Tom earlier.

I'd had the chance to pray for James and even mention Jesus' words to him, and it hadn't been weird in any way and yet I had nothing to show for it. I wasn't going to meet James again. He wasn't going to come to church, or to any kind of group. I hadn't given him a New Testament or any information to help him answer questions. I had hardly said anything and had let him go without any sort of attempt at a gospel presentation or follow-up. For a moment I was tempted to decide that I was going badly wrong with the whole mission thing. Perhaps, I thought, if I couldn't take things a bit further with people I spoke to, I shouldn't really be leading a team. Perhaps I shouldn't be on the mission at all?

I had, however, learnt to offer thoughts and feelings like these straight to God – if I didn't want to be paralysed by them for the rest of the week, that was. So I prayed, and as I prayed I was reminded once again that the mission was simply about playing a part in God's plan. It wasn't about meeting a set of measurable goals and aims.

I'd been in the right place at the right time for James to come and speak to me. I had offered the conversation to God as it began so it would be reasonable for me to trust that God was right in the centre of our brief, simple exchange. How could I know what God had been doing in James' life up until that point? And how could I know what else he would do?

I couldn't.

I was learning that if I were willing, God would use me in odd ways – ways that might make absolutely no sense to me at all. He can use us in any way from a smile to a stranger to a lifelong friendship full of shared experiences and profound conversations.

My lot was not to scurry round, trying to ram the gospel into conversations, get positive responses and fill in follow-up sheets. I simply needed to be concerned with being open to God and ready to act as he directed – even if that meant taking a risk. It was a lesson I would be reminded of again and again that week.

Beach Mission?

The rhythm lifted and thumped. Around the circle hands went up. Praises sang out to God: random, indistinguishable sounds. Words shouted and whispered. Eyes closed. Hands clapping. Tongues praising. Sound building. Hands beating. Energy lifting. Together. Worshipping God. Together.

God was in our midst. We were together. God was with us.

It was our third night as a team. Dinner had been wolfed down and we'd gathered in a circle to pray. No one had expected more than an average, calm(ish) time of chatting to God. But the whole thing had just taken off; I wasn't sure quite how. One thing had led to another and before we knew it, God's Spirit had moved us from simple prayers into unexpected territory. We had shared a rare closeness with God and with each other and could sense ourselves being knit together as a team.

Around the circle, the guys began to open their eyes, climb to their feet, stretch and smile. A dynamic energy filled my chest. As I looked around at the unlikely group – none of whom had given up, in spite of my earlier doubts – I thanked God for a great team.

I was excited about what the coming evening might hold for us. The rumour of a plan was circulating. At various points during the previous evening, every team member had walked past Towan beach and noticed that it was packed with hundreds of partygoers.

Half of my team had gone down for a closer look and hadn't returned to the basement until after 3am. I'd been impressed that they'd still made it along to the daily Dawn Patrol worship session only six hours later! They'd got into some great conversations on the sand and were adamant that we should all go back the following night.

We put it to the vote. It was unanimous. We

would split into smaller groups to work in bars to kick off and then meet up on the beach after midnight.

I was happy with the plan but had promised Rachel that I would spend some time with her and Hannah. It felt like a dilemma. Finding a suitable balance between "team" and "family" seemed more difficult than I had expected during my pre-mission planning.

I needed to keep my promise to Rachel. That meant that the team would have to go out without me.

The guys were chatting excitedly, pulling on their Dawn Patrol t-shirts and hoodies, getting the drums ready to take out and stuffing pockets with questionnaires and tracts. They were proving focused and more than capable.

I pulled Sophie, the team's pastor, to one side and explained my decision. She was tying back her hair and tucking it into her hoodie but still listened with keen, interested eyes. She was sucking a peppermint and offered me one as I told her that I couldn't do that evening and would she mind taking responsibility for the team in my absence.

"Not at all," she said matter-of-factly. "Go and be with Rachel and enjoy it!" She beamed generously.

I took the mint she was holding out and plopped it in my mouth, relieved. If possible, I added, I would join them on the beach in the early hours. Sophie smiled and nodded firmly. She had been in the group who had been down on the beach with the party the night before.

"You should definitely try if you can," she declared with a conviction that intrigued me. "It's worth seeing!"

As I leapt up the wooden steps from the basement two at a time, I resolved to get to the beach in the early hours to see things for myself. I wanted to play my part with the team in what God had planned for the clubbers on the beach.

The Lost Carnival

After an evening spent chilling with Rachel, I set off from the flat for Towan beach to hook up with my team. The moment I arrived, I realised that I'd left my phone behind and that finding the team was going to be like trying to meet up with a mate at Glastonbury... (almost impossible). Hundreds of people had spilled onto the sand from the town's bars and nightclubs. The beach was bursting into chaotic life like an algae-bloom in a pond.

In the drunken chaos of the beach party I felt out of place and uninvited. My mind swelled with self-consciousness about the red hoodie I was wearing which, I imagined, announced as loudly as a trumpet that I was a Christian and therefore naïve and judgemental.

Awkwardness, brought on by the fact that I knew I was on the beach for a different reason to everyone else, clouded my steps. A discouraging nag in my head whispered that I was like an unwelcome salesman or worse, a predatory shark. I was having trouble imagining how I might speak to anyone that night in any kind of normal way that would make sense.

I needed to find my team and the safety of being among familiar faces. Then perhaps I could think about why I was on the beach and begin to focus on how God might use me that night.

～

Drunk girls and lads stumbled and tripped, yelled and laughed. Empty bottles clanked and smashed under foot. Men in fancy shirts stood along the top of the beach wall with their arms outstretched, chanting at the crowds. Below them a continually shifting row of lads relieved themselves against the stones so that a stream of urine flowed across the sandy cobbles underfoot. A girl wearing high-heels lost her footing and crumpled onto the sodden ground. There were shrieks of laughter. She was hauled to her feet, unaware of the source of her damp clothes.

I stuffed my hands into the pocket across the front of my hoodie. My fingers met in the fleece lining. I looked around for a red top that I would recognise.

Nothing.

I pushed into the thronging mass, trying not to appear awkward or alone.

I was in unfamiliar territory. I felt out of my depth. Everyone around me was either drunk or high or both. The atmosphere was filled with confusion and tinged with fear. It felt out of control. I felt that anything could happen at any moment.

I swept my head from side to side, scanning for a red hoodie like a ship in fog seeking the beam from a lighthouse.

"Need any pills?" A wiry man dressed in a shabby, thigh-length leather coat aimed his remark surreptitiously as he padded past me.

I shook my head and turned to watch him as he continued on his way. He wandered over to a group of what looked like A-level students. They were bursting with drunken confidence. The dealer was masked from my view as they huddled around him.

Ahead of me a crowd had gathered around a fire made of rubbish. I looked at people's faces as I passed. Behind the joints and cans of lager, most of them seemed aimless – as if they were waiting for someone with a megaphone to announce what we were all doing next.

Flirting couples grabbed at each other, snogging before even asking one another's names. Hen and stag parties sprawled across the sand. Girls whooped and screeched. Men pulled moonys, students wrestled.

I felt as if I was at a bizarre carnival with no focus.

Just then, a group of young lads grabbed my attention. They were standing in a semi-circle around someone I couldn't see. They were having an unusually calm, almost sober discussion. I was fascinated and changed direction to get a better look. I was gob-smacked to discover Libby – the most studious, conservatively dressed member of my team – confidently addressing the whole group.

At that moment, a welcome, rhythmic thumping filled the air.

Drums!

Paul and Matt had to be close by. I crouched to look through the legs of a large group blocking my way. There they were; a small circle of red-hooded Dawn Patrollers sitting on the sand. Each was in conversation with a different person. It was a relief to find familiar faces.

As I reached them, Paul spotted me and raised a hand from his drum in greeting. Matt produced a peaceful grin. Angie, a feisty Lancashire lass, leapt to her feet. The two guys with whom she'd been chatting looked slightly startled.

"It's been mental down here, Mike!" she announced with broad arm gestures. "We've been in so many amazing conversations. God's been really good." She pulled her hands up into the sleeves of her hoodie before blasting on. "D'you know what? I reckon we need to pray about this properly, and then tomorrow night, right, we should get some of those garden flaming-torch things to give us more of a presence."

This sounded like a good plan. I looked towards Paul, who was drumming casually. He continued tapping out a beat while curling his tongue and considering Angie's idea.

"I was thinking perhaps we could give away free water," he suggested, focusing his gaze on my eyes. "No strings attached – just a way of blessing people. There's loads of people on drugs who should be drinking water but the only thing any-one's selling is cans of lager – we'd be helping them out."

This was a great idea. For the remaining nights of the mission we would create a tiny beacon in the centre of a dark, pointless party. We would set up camp in the middle of the action, where God could use us. And we would pray. We would begin to pray like none of us had prayed before and we'd be persistent in our prayers because around us was a vast crowd of souls who needed God to come to the rescue, even if none of them knew it.

Prayer Sneak

On our second night on the beach as a team, we found a spot just off centre and out of reach of the gradually advancing tide.

Along the length of the beach people were run-ning into the sea. I stood watching and noticed a pattern. First, clothes were thrown onto the wet sand, followed by a naked charge towards the inky blackness of the Atlantic ocean. As people ran towards the water, they disappeared from view – the light from the buildings on the cliffs above couldn't penetrate the darkness. There was shrieking for a few minutes until they re-emerged to begin the chilly and often unfruitful search for their clothes – which had inevitably been removed by practical jokers or thieves.

It struck me that if any of the swimmers got into trouble they stood zero chance of being rescued. No one could see them and everyone was busy being drunk. I asked the team, who were scattered around me to offer up some hefty prayers for their safety.

The beach was beginning to fill up as the clubs kicked people out. Around the spot that we had chosen to settle ourselves, five stubby garden torches protruded from the sand, their paraffin flames grabbing at the air. Paul and Matt tapped out a gentle rhythm on the drums. We had forty-eight bottles of water with us to give away. I wondered if we would have any takers.

A group of lads passed behind us. Sophie and Angela were on their feet, hands clutching bottles of water.

"Free water anyone?"

The lads changed direction and gathered around the girls. The water disappeared into grateful hands. A conversation began to sprout from the lad's confusion over the "free" part of free water.

We had attached neat little fold-out leaflets to the necks of the bottles. They prompted the reader to ask "What's your passion?" and explained God's passion for us.

Sophie told the group that the only condition of taking the water was to read the leaflet. One of the lads spoke out with sudden recognition.

"I know you lot!" He sounded surprised.

Paul and I turned around.

"You're the Christians that organise the football!" His outburst prompted some of his mates into recollection.

"You're Dawn Patrol aren't you?" one of them chipped in, much to my amazement. The sports team had clearly made an impact.

There were smiles and handshakes all round and suddenly they were sitting down with us among the flaming torches.

It hadn't occurred to me before but there was a nice symmetry about the sports team and the clubbing team working on the same beach with the same people. I'd imagined us as lone rangers because we only had the night shift. But others began when we went to bed. God was working around the clock with the partygoers.

I began to talk to a young guy who had sat down beside me. He told me that his name was Zac and explained that he and "the boys" were a cricket team and they were out to get hammered. He didn't seem to be particularly hammered to me. I asked if he'd had a good evening to which he nodded unconvincingly before spinning things around and asking me about the mission.

Zac already knew that the team and I were Christians and he was eager to ask questions about what our faith involved. As we began to talk about God, the conversation took a serious turn. Zac had something weighing on his mind.

"I'm really frightened of dying." He spoke softly, clearly keen for his mates not to hear.

"It terrifies me. I think about it all the time." His brow furrowed.

I wanted to reach across and give him a hug. Reassuring words filled my mind. I kept quiet and prayed silently instead. He needed God to speak to his soul, not me trying to cheer him up. I wondered if my silent prayers would cause such a major thing to happen.

"Doesn't dying scare you?" he went on.

I thought for a moment, aware that he was studying the side of my face carefully.

"I'm not afraid of dying." I turned my head to look at him.

His mouth fell open a little and his eyes dropped in disappointment.

I ground my feet through the damp sand, forming two shallow troughs. I wanted to say something that would help. Several possibilities suggested themselves but none seemed exactly right.

"I trust God," I offered eventually.

"But how do you *know* he exists? There's no proof – what if there's nothing there?" Zac motioned at the sky with one hand and slapped the sand beside him almost aggressively with the other.

It was a fair question. I'd asked it myself many times. I thought for a moment and decided to offer him the answer I had arrived at after some serious wrestling.

"When I look at the world, and at myself, and at all these people on the beach," I swept my hand back and forth, "and I see how complex it all is, it's obvious to me that someone was responsible for it."

I paused before going on but didn't look at Zac. Instead I gazed out at the blackness where I knew the sea was.

"Everything works too well for it to be a giant accident."

"But what if it just *is* an accident?" Zac held his hands up, turning the palms face-up, level with his shoulders. "Maybe we are completely alone." His words were louder than they had been and they sounded despairing. The subject had made him forget his mates for a moment.

I tipped my head from side to side in consideration. He was waiting for me to defend my corner.

"For me," I was considering my words carefully, "it would take more faith to believe that God doesn't exist than to believe he does."

I'd come to realise that I believed in God because to deny his existence flew in the face of overwhelming evidence. For me, to dismiss God and pretend he didn't exist would entail making a daily decision to live in a fantasy of my own creating. All very cosy but a bit pointless in the long run. . .

"Perhaps you're as scared as me and you just *want* God to be real?" Zac suggested tactfully.

"All I can say is that I'm not interested in believing something that's a lie."

I reached down between my legs, scraped up some damp sand and rubbed it between the palms of my hands.

"I believe in God because I *know* he's real, not because I *want* him to be real." I sat forward, dropped the sand and dusted my hands together almost expressively, as if to emphasise the weight of my argument. "Sometimes I think it would be easier if it wasn't true. What's there to be afraid of if there is no God and nothing after this life? You die and that's that. You live your life and then you don't exist. That's easy!"

Zac took a sip from the bottle of water in his hand. I prayed again silently, asking God to keep me on track. Zac needed hope. I had hope. I wanted to communicate it properly. Another thought came to mind:

"The other thing that helps me believe in God," I made my tone lighter than it had been, "is the fact that we've got a conscience."

Zac's forehead wrinkled, lending him an expression of deliberate puzzlement.

"How does that prove there's a God?"

"Well, if we're some big accident then why do we have a conscience? What's that all about?"

"Your conscience is just your mind working." Zac pronounced the words with false care as if I was a bit simple and had missed something blatantly obvious. I could sense, however, that the thought was taking him into new territory.

"It's not!" I raised my voice but kept a friendly tone. "Your conscience tells you if you're doing something wrong even when your mind has decided to do it anyway. Deep inside you know there is a right and a wrong – we all do. Why's that?"

"It's just common sense – some things are right and others are wrong. . ." He didn't sound convinced with his own argument.

"But why? And *how* do we decide which is which? Why should something inside us tell us what's right and what's wrong?"

Zac chewed a nail, mulling over the thought.

"In my opinion," I said, "it's because there is a creator who has a sense of right and wrong and he has built a conscience into us to point us towards him."

Zac stopped chewing his nail but remained silent. He seemed to become aware of his mates again and looked around slightly anxiously – to see if any might have overheard our exchange. They were all in conversations with Dawn Patrollers. He gave them another sweep just to check none might be listening to what he was about to say and then he bent close to me and said quietly:

"I have to admit that sometimes I pray. . ." He

returned to his original position with a furtive glance around as if he had just confessed to doing something illegal.

". . .But none of my mates know."

I understood. Mates can be very quick to spot something they could have a laugh at.

"Do you think God listens to me?" The words were earnest – almost desperate.

"God is listening the whole time – he loves to listen to us." I spoke with as much conviction as I could gather.

Zac's reply was blatantly honest.

"I don't feel like he's listening. I don't feel anything. It's like I'm speaking at nothing. Surely if he's there, he can make me feel something – or give me some kind of sign?"

I knew how frustrated Zac was. We judge everything by our feelings. We know something's real when we feel it, so we assume that if we don't "feel" it's because there's nothing there.

I had begun to understand that it's not fair for us to apply the "feeling" logic to God. Feelings are not the right tool for detecting God. God just *is* whether we can feel him or not. I had learnt not to base my faith in God on my feelings because my feelings were always changing.

I did my best to explain this to Zac. He seemed

to understand although I wasn't sure it was the answer he was looking for.

I had a thought.

"Can I pray for you quickly, now?" I asked as matter-of-factly as I could. I didn't want to freak him out.

It seemed like the natural thing for me to do though – not awkward or weird. Zac and I had probably just had a more profound conversation than he'd had with any of his mates all week – maybe even ever. So what was a quick prayer between us?

"If you want. . ." He drew his legs up slightly, obviously feeling a little self-conscious. But I felt self-conscious too. I would just have to go for it.

I kept my eyes open and stared at the sand while uttering simple words. They were just loud enough for both of us to hear.

I thanked God for a good conversation and asked him to make himself real to Zac over the next few days, to protect him and bless him and take away his fear of death and give him hope in its place.

When I'd finished, Zac thanked me. We shook hands and he began to stand up.

At that moment one of his mates joined us.

"You've been ages. What've you been talking about?" He sounded excited and sincere.

Zac looked at him without speaking.

"Praying," I declared, standing up. Zac shot me an uncomfortable glance.

"I bet," I gestured across the crowded beach, "that if you got each of these people on their own and asked them if they had ever prayed, ninety-nine per cent of them would admit that they'd done it at least a few times."

The two lads looked around the beach and then back at me. Zac kept silent but his mate had something surprising to say in reply.

"Yeah, definitely!" he smiled matter-of-factly.

"I pray all the time," he added.

Drugs Bust

The team stared at me, grins beginning to form on their faces, as what I had suggested sank in. It was 4am. We had just rolled back to the basement from the beach.

"We should do it!" Sophie smiled at me with her eyes – her mouth was obscured by a cup of steaming peppermint tea.

The others, scattered among their sleeping bags, voiced their agreement.

That was that then: We would pray and ask God to prevent dealers bringing any drugs onto the beach the following evening (Wednesday).

Ecstasy, acid and weed were a massive part of Newquay's night life. At times over the previous nights, the beach had felt oppressive. Drugs had a lot to do with that.

Praying that there wouldn't be any was a tall order. The likelihood of there actually being *no* drugs at all on the beach the following evening was tiny. Newquay was awash with drugs. But God is a big God and all of us sitting in the basement knew, in theory at least, that nothing is too difficult for him.

So we prayed there and then and put the outlandish request to God.

And then, because it was getting light outside and none of us had yet had the chance to sleep, we crashed out.

When we rolled out of bed again a few hours later, we prayed again. A lot.

We weren't trying to convince God – I reckoned God had prompted us to pray about the drugs in the first place. Our prayers were our part of working alongside God on *his* plan.

Wednesday evening arrived and we prayed some more.

Eventually midnight passed and it was time to make our way to the beach. We pulled on our red hoodies, gathered up flaming torches and bottles of water to give away and headed out into the night to find out what God was doing.

Got Any Pills?

People had been asking us for drugs all week. Wednesday night was no different.

We hung out on the sand talking and at regular intervals people crouched down and asked if we had Es or weed to sell. But there was a difference.

No one had asked us if we wanted to *buy* any drugs and we had been on the beach for over an hour.

Every other night dealers regularly wandered past quietly offering pills. It was a normal part of each night. Everyone on the beach expected to be able to score if they wanted to.

Not on that Wednesday night though.

Another hour passed and still no one offered any of us drugs. I was beginning to consider allowing myself to believe that God had done something huge.

Interruptions from desperate clubbers became more frequent:

"Has any one got any pills? No? Come on, if you've got some. . . No? This is a joke man! The beach is dry. No one's got anything – not even a bit of hash!"

By 3.30am I was deep in conversation with a young couple. Every so often I had to look up and offer people what, to my amusement, had become a standard reply: "Sorry, no pills. . ." As time wore on I began to add: "And you probably won't find any either. . ."

In over three hours no one had offered any of the team drugs. Requests, however, were at record levels. I was pretty certain there actually were no drugs on the beach.

The situation was remarkable. The chances of this happening were similar to going to the post office and not being able to get a stamp – it just wouldn't happen. Unless, that was, God had done something extraordinary – which he seemed to have done on the beach that night.

A girl in orange hot-pants knelt beside me and the couple I was chatting with. As she did so, she overheard part of our conversation. God and sex had been mentioned in the same sentence. She stood up immediately and dropped a disapproving frown down on the three of us.

"You're Christians, right?"

"*I'm* not!" protested one of the students. "No offence," she added, touching my arm reassuringly. I smiled at her sympathetically.

"No point asking you for pills then," the hot-panted girl concluded.

"No point in asking *anyone*," I leant back and rested on my elbows feeling unashamedly smug. The girl smirked at me contemptuously.

"There are no drugs on the beach," I stated. I was sure now, this was not merely a hope: it was a fact.

"Don't you worry about it," she announced defiantly, "I'll find some."

We'll see. . . I thought as she tossed her head and strode off among the sea of people.

Boat on the Beach

There were no drugs on the beach the following night either. In fact there was probably nothing and no one at all on the beach; it was pouring with rain.

With rain hammering down outside, we hung out in the basement debating a plan.

The following night (Friday) would be a big one in town. For many of the clubbers it would be their last before going home. They would want to make it a memorable one. The beach was likely to be at its busiest and we wanted to be there and on top form. It seemed that the best plan for us was having some good rest in preparation.

Before hitting the sleeping bags, however, we decided to spend a bit of time praying. It was a good decision – we would be glad we had.

We gathered in what had become our regular circle. Matt tapped gently on his drum. Paul gave us some chords on the guitar. We began to sing.

Singing grew into praying for each other. We took turns to stand in the middle and have the others pray for us. It was a habit we'd got into early in the week. At first we'd all been nervous and awkward but that had quickly disappeared. By the second day, asking for prayer and offering to pray had become as normal as making a cup of tea.

When it was my turn I sat with my eyes closed, my palms cupped in my lap in a gesture of receiving. Team members put their hands on my shoulders and arms. I waited quietly for God to refresh and inspire me through the prayers of my friends. At first the prayers came all at once – a babble of voices praying together. Gradually that was replaced by single voices. People described images and phrases that came to mind.

Praying this way was something I'd learnt from Jem the previous summer. Asking God for special words of encouragement or guidance or insight to share with each other was something we had practised. Jem had prompted us to ask God for these "words of knowledge" and not to analyse what came to mind too much. Instead, we would offer whatever it was to the group and they would decide whether it was from God or way off the mark.

My time of being prayed for came to an end. I was the last. As people began to stretch and stand up, however, Nick announced that he had something to share with the team. Everyone turned to him, interested to hear what he had to say. He had been unusually quiet during our prayers. We were about to find out why.

As we had been praying a vision had filled his mind. He began to describe what he had seen:

In the vision he'd been sitting alone on Towan beach. The sun was warming the sand and the tide was a long way out. In the distance he'd noticed a rowing boat that had been pulled up on the wet sand. He stood and began walking towards it.

As he got closer he could see that the boat was made of solid, heavy timber. He was still a little way off when he realised that it was much older than he'd first thought. It became apparent that it had been lying on the sand for many years. It was embedded. Nothing was going to move it. It would be there for years to come.

"I understood immediately what this picture was about," he explained to us as he finished describing what he had seen.

The team were listening in silence. His description had taken us all right there with him.

"Just like the boat, God has been on this beach for years," Nick went on softly. "God was here long before we came and will be here long after we've gone home."

It was a good reminder to keep our own efforts in perspective. God had tasked us in for that week but he had a plan for Newquay that was running 24-7.

"But I think there's a bit more to the picture than that. . ." He looked around the circle tentatively.

"I think God wants us to know that he will be with us on the beach tomorrow night in a different way to other nights."

"What do you mean?" Sophie's voice cut through the charged atmosphere.

"I don't know – it was just the way I felt as I was looking at the boat. It's as if tomorrow night is somehow going to be the most significant. . ."

Wide-boy Toby

Friday night had arrived. The town had gone mental. The alcohol and hormone-fuelled carnival was bigger, louder and brighter than on any other night of the whole week.

As the team and I made our way down the slip road to the beach it seemed to be common knowledge that the "Christians-in-the-red-tops" gave out free water. Eager hands and smiles and shouts of "Cheers mate!" intercepted us from all sides.

As the team reached the bottom of the slope, I was left behind. A group of guys dressed in their best pulling-gear wanted bottles of water. I handed them a couple from the 24-pack I was holding. One of them immediately cracked off the lid, pushed a pill in his mouth and swallowed. He grimaced and shook his head.

"Ugghhh!" he protested, sticking his tongue out. "Pills taste like bleach, man."

Our idea of the free water hadn't originally been to help people wash down Es. Still, it wasn't exactly a shock that that was how it was being used. People were spilling out of nightclubs, not Bingo halls.

He offered the bottle back to me.

One of his mates pushed him and shouted, "You cheeky git! He's not your mum." He pointed at me.

"Sorry mate." He turned to me and frowned overdramatically, shrugging his shoulders apologetically. "No manners. . ."

"It's fine," I insisted, offering him a bottle.

"Yeah, go on then. Ta." He took the bottle and tapped it on my chest.

"What's the free water about then? Nothing's free in this life."

He spoke with an east London accent, was in his late twenties and a little shorter than me. He was not particularly well built but his eyes, closely cropped hair and cocky manner told me that he probably wasn't a stranger to the odd pub-fight. He was wearing an expensive-looking Ben Sherman shirt that was half a size too large so that it hung loosely from his slim frame.

"You're right – the water isn't entirely free," I admitted.

"You can 'ave it back then!" He pushed the bottle back at me self-confidently.

I held a hand up to reject it and pointed at the little leaflet attached to the neck.

"You've just got to read that. . ."

He yanked the leaflet free and looked at it cautiously on both sides.

"What's your passion?" He read out the printed title and looked up wearing a wry smile.

"So this is all about God?" He waved the leaflet at me, "And you're down here to talk about God?"

"Yeah," I admitted almost hesitantly, wondering what his reaction might be.

He slapped me on the arm.

"It's good mate!" he yelled heartily, as if I had just given him a racing tip.

I was relieved.

"It's good that people like you give up your time to come and tell the rest of us about God. Personally I'm confused 'cos there's so many religions. It's nice to meet someone who knows what they think."

I assumed that having taken the water he would turn back to his mates. They had moved on down the slip road and were chatting up a couple of girls. Instead, he offered his hand and introduced himself:

"I'm Toby," he said, shaking my hand firmly.

"I'm Michael – it's good to meet you."

"It's good to meet you too Michael, but listen, right. . ."

I wondered what was coming.

"Do you seriously think God can do much good here? I mean, look at it, mate – everyone's off their boxes. No one gives a stuff about God."

The box of water was getting heavy. Praying silently about how to reply, I hoisted it up onto the wall behind me.

Just then, aggressive shouts caused us to turn our heads. My response would have to wait. There was trouble coming down the slip road.

Two young men were sprinting towards us. Toby moved quickly. The men tumbled past at full pelt. Terrified expressions were scrawled across their faces

A gang of lads in their late teens were in vicious pursuit. They were running like dogs – their faces screwed up with anger. My heart began to pump faster. They thundered past like a truck, screaming obscenities. They were faster than their prey. They would be on them in seconds.

I looked around for any sign of the police. There was none.

The first young men had reached the sand. The

crowd parted like a curtain to let them through. One of them caught his foot. He began to stumble. People continued to get out of the way. Everyone could see that something violent was about to kick off. No one wanted to get caught in it.

The stumbling man tried to steady himself but the gang was already descending on him. He fell down. Kicks and punches smashed into him. People shrieked in shock and dismay. I was rooted to the spot – horrified by what I was seeing but unable to help.

His friend sprinted on desperately but he had nowhere to go. Half the gang had followed him. He was surrounded. Punches and kicks reduced him to a heap.

No one knew what to do. Hundreds of people stood around while these two men took a beating. Everyone, including me, was too shocked and afraid to do anything.

And then, as quickly as it had started, it was over. The whole thing had lasted seconds. The gang came back together, swearing and spitting at the two battered heaps they had left on the sand. People looked away as they passed. The gang members were hyped. It wouldn't take much for them to start on someone else. They felt like big men – as if they were invincible rather than pathetic.

"Drugs," announced Toby confidently as the gang disappeared. He seemed familiar, even comfortable with what we had just witnessed, as if violence like that was an accepted part of his life.

"Those boys are dealers," he went on. "I've seen them round the town. It's a dark world mate." He pointed down at the sand where the young men lay groaning and shook his head, tutting unsympathetically. "Those two should have steered well clear."

People had gathered around the two victims. I was about to go and see if I could help when an ambulance and a police van appeared.

"So, could God've stopped that happening then?" Toby was still at my side and he gestured at the sand again, interrupting my thoughts.

I turned to look at Toby's face. Although there was a note of facetiousness in his voice, he wanted a real answer.

"God *could* have stopped it," I replied. "But if God stepped in every time something bad was going to happen, what kind of world would that be?"

"One where nothing bad ever happened!" His retort was sarcastic. "If God's got the power to stop bad stuff happening, he must be a sadist not to do it!"

I disagreed. "He's not interested in having billions of robots all programmed to do the right thing though is he? Obviously God *wants* us to choose to do what's right."

I shrugged and opened my eyes wide as if the point needed no explanation.

"I've done a lot of bad things in my life – *really* bad things – vicious stuff, you know? Like what just happened." He nodded towards where the paramedics were dealing with the two injured guys on the sand.

I wasn't sure why Toby had told me that. I had no idea about how to answer so I just continued to look him in the face inquisitively, waiting for him to add to what he'd admitted.

"I regret things I've done, man. I've messed people up – done damage. I reckon it would have been good if God had stopped me. . ."

All I could think to say was, "God lets you make your own decisions." I thought I sounded a bit lame.

I ran a hand across my head. Toby was treating the conversation as if it was a confession opportunity. I wasn't prepared for that. I hadn't got in the swing of the evening properly. I was still in a *where are we going to put ourselves on the beach tonight?* frame of mind. I prayed silently and wished that

God's voice was more audible at times like these. . .

"All the same," replied Toby, giving no indication that he thought my remark was a lame one, "I wish God had stopped me. I was out of control when I was younger – exactly like those geezers just now."

"Things can change," I offered.

"Yeah? How's that?" His head pulled back and his face tensed up. The frustration in his voice was blatant. "You think God can change me? I don't think so – he can't change what's happened either. . ."

"That's what Jesus was all about." I wasn't sure how he'd react to me dropping that name. Things were getting unexpectedly deep.

"*Jesus*! What's Jesus got to do with anything?" Toby stepped back and bumped into someone passing behind him. "Sorry geeze. . ." he offered without looking at them.

"It's *all* about him," I said, standing my ground. "Jesus came to tell us to stop doing wrong and get straight with God."

"My *mum* told me to stop doing wrong," laughed Toby. "It's not as easy as that though is it?"

"No offence," I replied, "but your mum isn't claiming to be God's son is she?"

"Don't talk about my mum!" warned Toby, half joking.

I decided to steer clear of future references to her.

"No, it's not easy," I admitted, scratching the back of my neck and pulling my bottom lip in for a moment. "My point is, Jesus claimed to be the son of God, and he said that whoever trusted in him would have a fresh start – a clean slate with God."

"And you believe that do you?" he shot back incredulously.

"Would I be talking to you about it if I didn't?" I asked him in reply. "I've got nothing to gain from telling you all this – I'm not on commission."

Toby pushed his hands into the back pockets of his trousers, looked at the ground and sighed.

"I need forgiveness man, I'm telling you. I've done some things that would mess your head up if I told you." He shook his head slowly from side to side.

I could only imagine what he might mean.

"Sometimes I feel sick with guilt," he went on. "I get twisted up." Then he paused. An idea slipped gently into my mind. If we could somehow get around to praying, I thought, God could do something profound in Toby's soul that would be far better than me chatting on. Time was pressing

185

though. I'd have to be quick. Toby could decide to leave at any moment.

"I need a leak, man," he announced abruptly. I read between the lines immediately. He wanted to get away but didn't want to offend me. I had blown my chance. Or perhaps I should just get the prayer in quickly? No: It was too late. He was already taking steps away from me. People passed between us. I was irritated with myself. The conversation had seemed to be going somewhere worthwhile but I'd let it slip away. I felt as if I'd let an opportunity slip away.

"Stay there! I'm coming back," he called over his shoulder as he disappeared.

I didn't believe him.

"Seriously mate, I'll be back – stay there!"

I decided I'd give him five minutes.

I stood watching the crowds and wondering how the rest of the team were getting on. The police were on the beach taking statements. The bulk of the crowd had shifted further down the sand. People wanted to carry on without worrying about getting busted.

Five minutes had gone and I was starting to feel embarrassed about standing around on my own when everyone else was with their friends. I felt like a billy-no-mates. The twenty bottles of water for giving away didn't help – it looked as if I'd brought them along to make friends!

The ambulance rumbled up the slope. I watched it go and got ready to shift the bottles of water from the wall.

"Alright geeze! Cheers for waiting – I was busting."

To my surprise Toby reappeared with an eager grin.

"It's been good to speak to you man," he said. "You're alright. A few years ago I would have smacked you in the face if you'd tried to talk to me about God."

He aimed a mock punch at me. I laughed.

"I'm serious." He pulled his fists back and bashed them together in front of his chest. "But that was then and this is now, and you've given me a lot to think about."

I had another chance. I didn't want him to go away and think *about* God, I wanted him to go away and get to *know* God.

I needed to go for it.

"Listen Toby, let me pray for you."

I'd said it.

"Mate! You can pray for me all you want," he replied with a laugh.

"No: Here. Now," I pushed on. "Just quickly."

He folded his arms, clearly slightly taken aback, but took the suggestion in his stride.

"What do we have to do?" he asked. "Close our eyes and put our hands together like at school?"

"Nah," I shook my head with a smile. "We'll just stand here and I'll speak to God. That's it. And no one'll know what we're doing."

"Go for it then mate – pray away!" He stepped closer to me. I was a little surprised but took it as a good sign. I took a deep breath and then went for it.

It was a good little prayer. At least I thought it was. The words flowed simply. I could sense God's presence in spite of the hubbub around us. I was glad I had taken the risk.

And so was Toby. As we looked up and I went to shake his hand, he took it, pulled me towards him and embraced me in a massive hug. I didn't know what to say so I just patted his back in a manly fashion.

We parted with enthusiastic goodbyes, loud thankyous, several handshakes and an exchange of contact details. It was important that someone could get Toby more information about the things we'd talked about, and that he could get in touch with a Christian if he wanted to talk things through some more.

As he disappeared into the crowds, I silently committed Toby to God.

God had done so much it was hard for me to believe that the night had only just begun but already God was at work. I headed down onto the sand clutching my box of water bottles. As I began to look for the team I remembered Nick's vision of the boat that reminded us that Jesus was on the beach. I wondered what else God had in store that night.

Dawn Patrol

Dawn was beginning to break before my team finally gathered themselves together and made their way off the beach. The debris of the night lay all around us: bottles, cans, fag packets and other questionable bits and bobs. Each of us felt exhausted but jubilant. Our heads were bursting with stories of God-soaked encounters. As we kicked through the sand, we shared some of our stories – babbling away in twos and threes. There had been so many natural, cringe-free opportunities to share the fact that Jesus is alive. A stack of people had heard that knowing him makes a difference and that it didn't matter who they were or whether their life was messed up or ticking along nicely.

The openness we had encountered had been phenomenal. Most of the people we had spoken to were hungry for spiritual experience and many of them for something even deeper. There had been so many questions. No one on the team had all the answers but all of us had real relationships with the real God. God had used us and spoken through the things we had said, and people would be different that day because we had been on the beach and been prepared to talk about our faith.

I looked around at my team; tired, hungry, red hoodies beginning to hum. I had been wrong to judge these people by their appearance. God had hand-picked each one of them. As we walked back to the basement the sense of community was palpable – like thick ropes knitting us together.

I thought of Rachel and Hannah. Soon they would be waking up and packing, ready for us all to head home later that day. It would be good to get back to spending proper time as a family together.

Rachel had heard snippets of stories from my week and she'd hung out with the team during some of the afternoons. I wondered what she would make of the fact that as we climbed the slip road some members of the team were already talking about coming back again the following summer. The prospect of returning to Newquay excited me.

As a yellow glow seeped around the edges of the sky, announcing the coming day, I had the same feeling inside myself that I'd had the year before. I knew I would be coming back.

The beach would fill up with clubbers again on the following night as usual but we'd have gone home. As far as I knew there would be no one there to speak to anyone about God – no one to share anything deeper and more hopeful than a spliff or a few pills.

We were leaving but God wasn't. We had come to the end of a week of mission but God hadn't. He had people everywhere – tucked into the most surprising situations. He would be carrying on. Nevertheless, I could already sense the invitation to return and join in once again the following summer.

If I or any of the team was going to come back, however, it would be under different circumstances. There was no Dawn Patrol mission planned for the following summer. Andy Frost and the guys who had organised it were committed to hosting part of a massive mission due to take place in the summer in London called Soul in the City. It would require all their efforts so Newquay was off the agenda for them.

If I wanted to come back to Newquay to join God on the beach, I would have to find another way of doing it.

I could barely believe what I was contemplating as, having left my team at the church hall, I walked up the steps to the front door of my flat in the thin, early morning light. The idea of me bringing a mission team to Newquay on my own the following summer was so bizarre that it almost made me laugh out loud. *A mission team organiser? Me?* It sounded like a joke.

As I pushed the key into the lock and turned it, I offered the idea to God.

I stepped into the dim, silent hallway with its swirl-patterned carpet and pile of junk mail shoved against the wall. The idea might have sounded like foolishness but I knew that my God was full of surprises. He seemed to enjoy turning sense on its head and bringing something out of nothing. Perhaps the idea of me leading a mission team to Newquay the following summer wasn't so unlikely after all.

PART 3

God Bless Ibiza

"You've got to come and see this Michael!"

Rachel was calling to me from the living room. I was washing up in the kitchen of our home in London.

"There's something on TV about Christians in Ibiza," Rachel continued.

I dropped the plate scrubber into the soapy water and went to have a look.

For the next hour the washing-up was forgotten while I sat on the sofa, getting increasingly excited, as I watched a documentary about an organisation called 24-7 Prayer who had sent a team of young people to Ibiza for the summer to do exactly what I had recently returned from doing in Newquay.

As I watched, an idea began to form in my mind that I almost didn't dare to acknowledge. I was eager to return to Newquay with a mission team the following summer but with no Dawn Patrol mission planned, it was difficult to see how it could happen. Was it too much to suppose that 24-7 Prayer might be prepared to send me with a team to Newquay? Newquay was after all, not dissimilar to Ibiza – in fact Newquay was a popular second choice for thousands who couldn't afford the flight to Ibiza!

My mind was racing by the time I returned to the plates stacked in the now cold, sud-less water in the sink. As I waited for the water to run hot again, the mission-team idea ballooned in my mind like expanding foam. The more I thought about it, the more convinced I became that if I contacted 24-7 Prayer and suggested the idea of their sending a team to Newquay, they would go for it. I could even offer to organise the details and links with local churches and possibly even lead the team myself!

I needed to get online, find the 24-7 Prayer website and send them an e-mail, and I needed to do it at that moment! I abandoned the washing up for the second time that evening and tumbled upstairs to my study.

The prospect of my idea becoming reality thrilled and daunted me – so much so that although I was aware that it should be carefully prayed about, all I could manage was a sincere but hasty appeal for guidance as I waited for my modem to dial up the connection. I was trusting in the somewhat mistaken logic that God *had* to be behind my plan because I was certain I wouldn't feel quite so excited about it if he wasn't.

Chuffed

24-7 Prayer replied to my e-mail the following day and made it clear that sending a mission team to Newquay the following summer was a possibility that they would consider.

I re-read the e-mail, just to make sure I hadn't misunderstood it and that what 24-7 Prayer had actually said was that my idea was a possibility they'd *never* consider in a million years.

It was OK. I'd understood correctly.

I gave the air beside me an uppercut of delight and yelled an elated: *"Yes!"*

I leant back in my office chair and tapped my thumbs together feeling wanted and chuffed with myself. I'd responded to a stroke of inspiration and it had paid off. I wondered why I didn't try shot-in-the-dark things like this more often. . .

The e-mail from 24-7 Prayer explained that they could only give a proper thumbs-up once we'd met and talked through the concept in depth. Given what I'd seen in the Ibiza documentary, I couldn't imagine what they might possibly object to. I was certain our meeting would be a straight-forward formality.

A telephone number hung at the bottom of the message. The name beside it was "Ian Nicholson".

The e-mail said I was to give him a call to arrange a meeting.

~

I sat alone in a large, slightly tatty chair in Ian Nicholson's Guildford office, holding a mug of steaming coffee firmly with both hands and telling myself that there was absolutely no need to feel anxious. I reassured myself that the mission-team idea was a good one and not a waste of everybody's time.

A young woman poked her head and a single hand around the office door. She smiled and wiggled her fingers in what I took to be a friendly wave, and told me that Ian would be along any minute.

Once she'd gone I tried to relax. I wanted to appear confident and together and capable of leading a mission team. I wanted it to be patently obvious to Ian that I was made of mission-team-leading-stuff. Inside, however, I felt like a fraud. My mission experience was limited to two weeks – two *dramatic* weeks – but only two weeks, nevertheless. I wondered if I had perhaps been a bit naïve in approaching 24-7 Prayer and offering to organise and lead a mission team with them.

I didn't have any more time to worry about it though. As my eyes flicked over the books on Ian's busy shelves, the office door swung open and in walked Ian clutching a large mug of coffee and offering a warm greeting.

He dropped into his chair – the leather let out a sigh – and we began to talk.

It soon became obvious to me that Ian and I understood each other pretty well. Ian's passion about God and mission excited me and my ideas appeared to enthuse him.

By the time an hour had passed he'd given me the provisional thumbs up to organise and lead a mission team with the backing of 24-7 Prayer. My lack of experience wasn't an issue. The following summer, all being well, I would be leading a small team of Christians to pray, serve and talk about Jesus in Newquay.

Before we parted company, Ian and I prayed and committed the whole project to God. It was the first time I'd really focused on asking God for his opinion about the mission team. Everything had moved so quickly and, as is too often the case, prayer had been the first casualty. I resolved to change that. If the team was going to happen, prayer needed to be at the top of my agenda.

As we said our goodbyes, Ian and I hugged. (A manly hug. . . we'd only met an hour before!) I took it as a good sign.

Dear Young Evangelist. . .

The months passed quickly, a new year arrived and before I knew it, August was only weeks away and my mission team consisted of three "possibles" and me.

In Ian's office the previous September, we'd talked about the team being fifteen-strong. That had since dropped to ten and it was looking like it might have to drop to five, although even that didn't look too likely! I told myself that five was fine. Five would be good. . .

I didn't believe my own hype though. Five was rubbish.

In my phone calls and e-mails to Ian, who was busy sorting out decent-sized teams going off to places like Ibiza, Aiya Nappa and Belgrade, I began to slip in subtle hints of possible termination. I wanted to prepare him for the high probability of my pulling out and dropping the idea of taking a team to Newquay. With such little interest, I couldn't see how it could work.

I was beginning to wonder if perhaps my excitement had clouded my thinking and the whole idea had just run out of control and far away from God's interest.

I sat at my desk, looking out of the window at the school playing field behind my house. My hand was on the telephone receiver. I would call Ian and tell him Newquay was off. I paused for a moment. It would be better to tell him by e-mail, I thought – the coward's way. . .

I opened my e-mail account. Waiting for me was a message from 24-7 Prayer. It read: "Two team members paid. References in the post to you."

~

It was only two people but they were definitely coming. I was so encouraged by the news that I decided to postpone contacting Ian and redouble my prayer efforts. And I decided to stop worrying that perhaps my mission-team idea had been conceived in a moment of egotistical rashness.

I recalled the memory of leaving the beach for the last time the previous summer and knowing inside myself that it was important to return. If those feelings had been inspired by God in some way – and I believed they had – then I felt sure I could trust God to supply everything needed for the imminent mission – in this case a team of young(ish) evangelists.

Two days later an e-mail arrived from Paul and his brother Matt – the drummers from the previous summer. They had seen the team advertised on the web and were writing to volunteer!

Including me, that made five of us. The mission was looking more plausible. Feeling encouraged once again, I made more phone calls and sent enthusiastic e-mails. I contacted anyone that I thought might be up for it. One by one, three more people agreed to join the team.

That made eight, which was OK but I felt like ten would be better. It seemed somehow more rounded and, well, there would be more of us. . .

There was a possibility. A couple I hadn't tried; Pete and Suzie. Pete was a youth worker like me and we'd taken a stack of high-school lessons together. He and Suzie could both sing, Pete could play the guitar and (very important) they were a good laugh. They didn't know it at that point, but they needed to be on the team.

Rachel and I invited them round for dinner. When the meal was over I slipped them the best sales pitch I could manage. I extolled the virtues of sleeping on the floor, sharing a single, grotty shower and having hardly any sleep. They left promising to think about it.

24-7 Prayer

Two days later my phone beeped. I opened the text message. It read: "Me n Suz cn mk it!"

It was brilliant news. Pete and Suzie hadn't been put off by the idea of sleeping on a wooden floor for a week, which meant the team would be ten. God had built something from not much (as usual).

I began to feel more positive and excited about the mission. The applications and references had been dealt with, the accommodation (church hall) was booked and road directions had been sent out with a rough outline of what we were likely to be doing during the mission. All I had left to do was get myself to Newquay.

On the way I dropped Rachel and Hannah in Falmouth. They would be staying with Rachel's parents and I would try to see them at some point during the week.

I arrived in the town on a Friday night in early August. My team weren't due to arrive until the following day. I wanted time to prepare the hall where we'd be staying, buy some food and have a wander round the town.

The hall, and the hulking Methodist church to

which it was attached, were built of large, sombre blocks of stone. The two buildings occupied an inconspicuous spot down a side street in the town centre. They were the type of edifices that it was possible to walk past without really noticing that they were there. (It was the same hall in whose dim, faintly damp basement my team had stayed the previous summer.)

That night I sat in the dusty wooden grotto that was the church hall with no TV or music to distract me from the fact that I was completely alone. Sitting among my surfboard, rucksack and sleeping bag on the bare floorboards, under the harsh glare of the hall's strip lights, I felt small and insignificant.

Worries and doubts about the week ahead crowded into my head. In previous years, teams I'd been part of were one of many in a much larger mission. The week of mission that lay ahead of my team that summer, however, would be a week spent entirely alone. I felt like we were embarking upon some kind of remote polar expedition.

I wondered if we were up to it. There was no big worship meeting with dynamic teaching to attend each morning. We would have to generate our own worship, prayer, working hours, eating arrangements and sleeping patterns. If it went wrong and we all fell out where would we go? (Home, probably...)

Suddenly the Ibiza documentary I'd seen back in my cosy home in London seemed a very long way away. Anxiety closed its chilly fingers around my mind and I began to worry that I'd cajoled the team members into agreeing to come along on what might turn out to be a completely naff mission. The whole thing seemed somehow rather pathetic – as if the guys who'd be arriving the following day were just indulging me.

What if they got bored and had a rubbish time and went home early thinking, *Michael's naff mission was a joke*?

I felt inadequate and alone.

As I sorted out the corner of the hall where I would sleep that night, I realised that I needed God's help. And I needed it at that moment.

I ceased pumping up my air-mattress and sat down instead on its half-full-of-air wobbliness. I put my head in my hands and I asked God to: Help! Help! Help!

As I sat in the silence after pouring out my impassioned request, I decided (again) to trust that the mission team had been God's prompting and that it would be neither naff nor boring.

I closed my eyes and allowed myself to know

that far from being alone and facing an insurmountable challenge for which I was ill-prepared and unqualified, I was in the company of my loving and infinitely capable heavenly Father. The week ahead was *his* week and he would prove trustworthy.

The Team

The first day of the mission dawned, bringing with it Paul Chowdry. His tiny Fiat bumped up the curb outside the church hall. He climbed out of the battered car looking shell-shocked. He'd had a long, and by the look of it, tiring journey from Birmingham.

"I can't believe you've made me come," were his first words. I hoped he was joking. I was still trying to keep the anxieties of the previous night at bay.

I was seriously pleased to see him. We'd become good friends since meeting and DJing together on the first summer of mission.

Paul would be the team's theological equivalent of heavy artillery. I remembered seeing him in action with the white witch during our first summer in Newquay. When he was speaking to people about Jesus, he had an incredible knack for seeing right to the core of what was behind their arguments. He could spot a person's motivation, pursue it relentlessly and bring it out into the open like a spiritual sniffer-dog. He'd ask demanding questions and somehow he managed not to get beaten up. Needless to say, his conversations with complete strangers often ended up being hours rather than minutes long. I was looking forward to watching him in action again.

The brothers, Matt and Paul, arrived next. They strode into the church hall, bedangled with rucksacks, sleeping bags and two large drums. I asked where their car was.

"We got the train," Matt announced, placing his drum carefully on the hall floor.

"It was badly delayed," Paul added, dropping his stuff in a heap beside Matt's drum. He rubbed his belly. "You got any food? I'm starving."

The pair of them gave off a positive glow that brought the hall to life. There were five years between them but they appeared as close as twins. They would be a potent combination when it came to leading the team in worship and keeping us all enthusiastic.

Lunchtime arrived and with it Pete and Suzie – desperate to escape the confines of their stuffy car.

They had spent hours in the queue to get into the town and then almost as long trying to negotiate Newquay's one-way system and find the hall. They'd made it though – all the way from London. I was relieved. I would appreciate the support of close friends when things got tough that week.

Angie from Preston arrived next – except she hadn't come from Preston. She had moved to Newquay since being on the team the previous summer and had joined Jem's church, Blaze. She was like a generator busting with enthusiasm and laughter and conversation. Her confidence in God and willingness to trust him whatever else was going on inspired me and filled me with hope for the week ahead.

It was dinnertime when Sophie's train finally dragged itself into the station. She was tired but smiling after a crawling twelve-hour journey from the Isle of Wight. Her attitude spoke volumes. If she could be in a good mood after that, she'd do well with whatever the week ahead would throw at her. She would be an excellent encourager and a strong support for the rest of the team.

The last two, Tim, a student, and Chris, a PE teacher, rumbled into town at midnight. The team and I spilled out onto the street to meet them. Chris's car was crowned with a sea kayak that was attached to the roof bars. The pair of them were full of laughter and on good form. After handshakes and big smiles all round, we helped them drag their boot-load of bags inside.

The team was assembled. As we sat around in the hall laughing and getting to know each other, I felt as if we were in the queue for a towering theme park ride. Anticipation crouched like a sprinter in the pit of my stomach. The ten of us were about to embark upon an extraordinary week – a week of adventure with God and each other. I looked around at the faces of the team members. God had called us together. I wondered what he had in mind for the week ahead.

Prayer Room

On Sunday morning the ten of us rolled along to Blaze church, whose meeting place was in the cavernous Springbok nightclub. It was an interesting experience, not least because as the service ended the bar at the front of the club opened and in strode fifteen large, hairy men dressed in women's swimwear. It didn't take long to deduce that they were a stag party making an early start on their day's drinking. The sight reminded me of the mad context we'd be working in that week.

When the team and I got back to the hall we decided to organise a space that we could use as a prayer room. Tucked away at one end of the hall was a small vestry. Four windows were set deep into the wall opposite the door. The glass was stained so that people from the street couldn't see in but we could hear everything going on outside. It was stuffed with dusty chairs and, inexplicably, four old gas fires. It did have carpet on the floor though, and with a bit of imagination we reckoned we could transform it into a space that felt intimate and inspiring. The ten of us set to work, shifting chairs, zooming round with an ancient vacuum cleaner and digging useful accessories out of our luggage.

By the time we had finished with the little vestry, it was a space that was ready for action, like a canvas primed and waiting for some paint. Our prayer room would be a place where we could focus on God – a kind of sacred space.

We'd filled the deep window alcoves with tea-lights and large candles. The tatty red carpet was dotted with thick sheaves of paper. Coloured pens lay in clumps. A blob of blue tac was plonked in the middle like a paper-weight.

The plan was that as we began to pray, and then to meet people out on the streets, we'd write names and places on the paper. These would be stuck around the walls as reminders to keep praying. In the centre of the floor was a small, simple wooden crucifix. It would be a constant reminder of what we had come to Newquay to do.

Stacks of people in our generation saw the cross as a morbid symbol wrapped up somehow with an irrelevant guy. We'd come to Newquay that week in response to this, to introduce the people we would meet to a fresh perspective that was pregnant with life. Our tools would be prayer and serving and, when invited, words. It would require patience, wisdom and faith.

Newquay was a melting pot – a place that young people travelled to from all over the UK, even the world, to go clubbing and get wasted. On that global podium, my little team would try their best to live out the fact that God is alive and well and had come to a town near them – the town they were in, in fact.

It was a daunting task to be reminded of by the six-inch wooden cross that sat on the scruffy floor of our little prayer room. But the empty cross is a symbol of hope – hope of change and hope of a future. And because that hope was alive inside us, the ten of us would step up to the challenge and see what happened.

Letter Bomb

The team were impatient to get started on whatever it was that God had lined up for us in Newquay. We figured that the major part of our task would be simple, faithful prayer – prayer for the town and everyone in it.

That first Sunday evening we headed out onto the rowdy streets to prayer-walk. We swept the town from the huge stone cross on the hill at one end, to the point where the buildings stopped and the road ran out of town at the other. We walked in silence, praying in our heads for the people stuffed into the streets around us.

The arcades jangled and blared and music boomed out of the packed bars. We wove to avoid drunken crowds and stationary doormen in the high street.

We passed along the road beneath the supermarket whose steps my team had sat down on the previous summer to pray. As we made our way towards the spot where we'd discovered Tom, I prayed silently: *Lord, give us clear directions. Show us what you want us to do in Newquay.*

Up ahead three young men, deep in conversation, were blocking the pavement.

I squeezed behind them, brushing my back against the wall of a cottage, and as I did so one of them exclaimed in an American accent: "I don't know whose got my back, man. I don't know *anyone* I can trust."

The remark was so heartfelt that a surprising compassion for the guy thumped me in the heart immediately. The guy didn't know whom to trust but *I* knew I could trust God. It wasn't a smug realisation. It was just a fact. I knew God had *my* back.

The team and I walked on leaving the little group behind but something inside me wasn't comfortable. We were heading out of town – towards Fistral beach. I felt like we were going the wrong way. I shouted to the team and suggested that we head back into the action. As we u-turned, the three guys were disappearing into the small cottage outside which they had been standing. The door slammed as we drew level. The team plodded on past but I hung back. Something inside me had been triggered by the American guy's comment about not knowing whom he could trust and I felt I needed to respond somehow.

I remembered that I had stuck a little booklet about God in the back pocket of my jeans before leaving the hall. I felt for it – it was still there. I wondered if perhaps I should stuff it through the letterbox of the cottage. Almost as soon as the idea occurred to me, it was followed by a torrent of reasons not to do it and I began to wrestle with myself.

The team had moved further ahead, leaving me dragging behind on my own. I prayed for guidance. It was just a booklet. Surely, I thought, it was no big deal to simply put it through a letterbox?

But by now I was way beyond the cottage. To post it meant running back. The situation began to feel silly. I prayed again: *What should I do Lord?*

As I prayed I looked up and experienced an odd moment straight out of the film *Bruce Almighty*. I found myself staring at a signpost that read "One Way". The arrow on the sign was pointing back the way I had just walked – back towards the cottage. I realised the dangers of interpreting a road sign in the way I was about to, but it made up my mind and I turned around and jogged back down the road towards the cottage.

The light from a street lamp illuminated the narrow wooden front door.

I had to pass the living room window to get to

the letterbox. I looked in through the net curtains. I couldn't see anyone. The coast was clear. I could deliver the booklet without looking like a weirdo and God could use it if he wanted to. I would remain anonymous but hopefully one of the guys would be touched by what they read and my conscience, pricked by the American guy's comment, would be eased.

I opened the flap of the letterbox and pushed the booklet through as quickly as I could. Then I turned and hurried away. I had only gone ten paces when behind me I heard the sound of a front door opening and a voice shouting at me.

Bunker Boy

"Dude!" someone with an American accent yelled, "What's *this*, dude?"

I turned around to face whoever was calling me and, not really knowing what to say, just smiled and replied:

"It's about you and God – read it!"

Then I turned and hurried on. Getting caught hadn't been part of the deal. I'd expected to be able to get clean away without looking like a well-meaning weirdo who sneakily pushes things into people's letterboxes after having heard snippets of conversations.

I made it to a car park just up the road where my team were milling around waiting for me. I didn't get to speak to them though. I could hear footsteps hurrying up behind me. I turned around to find the guy that had just shouted from the cottage doorway right there.

He was tall and clean-cut with keen blue eyes and he was smiling – which was good. At least I hadn't offended him with my sneaky God booklet and hasty follow-up introduction.

"Dude," he began, "what's with the booklet, man?"

It was a reasonable question but as I prepared to answer it I found myself being amazed that the guy had actually bothered to run after me for an explanation. It had only been a booklet through the letterbox after all. Back home in London I got things through the door all the time. I never ran after whoever put them through. . .

I explained the sequence of events that had led up to my putting the booklet through his door. He nodded, absorbed. I included everything – hearing his conversation, praying, seeing the "One Way" sign – the whole lot. I figured that as he was obviously interested enough to run after me, I might as well be up-front. He seemed to like it so I took the initiative and asked him about himself.

His name was Liam. He worked for the US Navy and was based in Newquay.

I hadn't known the US Navy had people based in Newquay!

What was really bizarre, however, was that his job, along with several hundred other Americans, was to monitor submarine movements in the Atlantic from inside a very deep, underground bunker. I hadn't known anything about any bunker! But then, Liam hadn't known anything about any mission team so we'd both learnt something new. . .

Liam didn't want to talk about the bunker though (not to mention the fact that he probably wasn't allowed to. . .). He steered the conversation back to what led up to my putting the booklet through his door, explaining that he was fascinated by the fact that I only had one copy and that he'd happened to be standing behind the door when it dropped through and that it was all about God. Basically, he loved the seeming randomness of it all set alongside the weight of it being about God.

"This is crazy," he tapped the side of his head with three fingers on his right hand, "because there's all these heavy thoughts about life and religion going through my head right now and then I meet you. . ." He shook his head as if it was all a little overwhelming and wiped a hand over the front of his loose, checked shirt.

He was right. It was crazy. I'd learnt from previous experience, though, that God was a regular expert at doing crazy stuff. I was excited rather than surprised. Excited that God had prompted me to do something that tapped into what he was already doing in Liam's life and that I had been willing (just) to take the risk of looking a bit weird.

I found the situation funny because I could see that God wanted to get Liam's attention – *I* knew that God was seeking Liam. Liam, however, thought that if any seeking was going on, it was being done by him, alone, in his own time and that he would reach his own conclusions, "thank-you-very-much".

But the thing was, God had already found Liam. It was just a question of how long it would take Liam to realise it. My part in the process was a brief, rather odd encounter. It would take other moments, conversations, revelations and random-seeming events but eventually, I had no doubt, Liam would recognise God's activity in his life and step towards him.

The conversation had a bit further to go. Liam wanted my opinion on a couple of hot topics. As a Christian, did I get high? And what did I think about sex?

I told him that I was married and thought sex with my wife was a great idea. He took a step backwards and laughed loudly. He didn't believe that I could possibly be married. Eventually I had to show him my wedding ring and tell him that I was thirty. He looked shocked.

"*Dude*! I would have said you looked twenty – max!"

I decided to take the comment as a compliment.

"No, I don't get high," I told him, "although I used to, years ago – until I realised that smoking weed just made me want to do nothing all day. . ."

Liam laughed again and slapped me on the arm, nodding his head as if he recognised the picture.

It was clear to Liam that as well as being a Christian I was a normal bloke – not because I'd smoked a bit of weed but because we'd laughed together and I'd answered his questions with common sense and not with naïve peachiness.

It was time for us to part company. He wanted to get back to his mates at the cottage and I needed to go and find my team – who'd slipped away during the conversation. As Liam and I shook hands and went our separate ways, I felt certain that our paths would cross again that week.

Night Shift

Assembled in the prayer room later that night, the team prayed for Liam.

Scattered candles cast warm, dancing shadows on faces and walls. Paul and Matt were tapping out a gentle rhythm on their drums. A CD played softly. We were in God's presence – waiting and listening for him.

People passed noisily on the street outside, unaware that as they did so we were praying for them.

Midnight passed and I began to think about sleep.

As I was about to mention the idea to the team, however, Suzie stood up and made an announcement that would increase the focus and spiritual temperature of the entire week:

"I'm going to be in here, praying till 4am."

Everyone looked at her in a way that told me I hadn't been the only one thinking about my sleeping bag. No one spoke – I guessed no one, including me, wanted to seem like a lightweight.

"I just think this is where God wants me," Suzie smiled. She'd obviously spotted the but-I-want-to-go-to-sleep look in all our faces. "We *are* supposed to be representing 24-7 Prayer after all."

She had a good point.

"And I think we should start as we mean to go on," she placed the palms of both her hands flat on the floor, "and it might be a bit of a sacrifice but if we're not prepared to do that then why have we come here?"

It was a challenge to all of us. I felt convicted because I'd certainly wanted to hit the sack but I also felt a tiny bit concerned about whether it should have been me rather than Suzie doing the challenging. I wondered if I was being slack. Did Suzie speak up because I'd failed to? Would the rest of the team have spotted the failure and begin to lose faith in my ability as a team leader?

I closed my eyes briefly and told myself to shove the insecurities out of the way. I needed to feel confident and accept Suzie's challenge with humility.

A ripple of acknowledgment that Suzie's words were right went round the room. Prayer was why we were in town. Praying that God would impact our generation was what we had come together to do, so we would all join her. We would do the night shift and begin to pray like people who meant business for the students, clubbers, surfers, skaters, goths, punks, townies, scallies, dealers and homeless who were heaped up in Newquay like a writhing, aimless army.

We prayed until long after 4am. Eventually we rolled into our beautiful sleeping bags and slipped into welcome unconsciousness. We had set ourselves a standard for the week but we'd only just begun. Bed before 4am would soon become a rapidly fading memory.

Nosedive

The night following Suzie's challenge, things became very bleak for me.

Half of the team took flaming torches and free water down to the beach with the aim of getting stuck into conversations in the middle of the beer-soaked mayhem.

Pete, Suzie, Paul Chowdry, Tim and I remained in the prayer room where, updated by text messages from our teammates, we could pray for them non-stop.

I was feeling tired when we began but it wasn't

long before tiredness was starting to develop into something more serious. I tried to shake it off by draining a large glass of water and stretching my arms and legs but my head was pounding. My limbs quickly grew leaden and my ribs ached. I rubbed my temples, struggling to massage away an increasing weariness.

I looked around the candlelit prayer room. Tim was kneeling in a corner, his eyes closed. Paul was reading something from the Bible and Suzie was writing. I looked at Pete and was a little perturbed to find him staring straight back at me with a fixed gaze. Usually I would have smiled or acknowledged him in some way but right then I couldn't. I was feeling worse by the moment. I dragged my eyes down towards the floor.

It wasn't just my body that ached. I realised that I had a throbbing emotional and spiritual ache too. I couldn't understand why this was happening.

I ran a hand over my head, pushed my back hard against the wall and closed my eyes. As I did so, I knew that I didn't want to be there. My heart dropped like a stone thrown down a well. I wanted to go home. The fact of being separated from Rachel and Hannah loomed inexplicably like a dark canyon in my mind and heart. A vicious swathe of bitter heartache washed over me like a cold, murky wave. It was as if I was being attacked from the inside. Nothing like it had ever happened before. I couldn't think properly.

I remained in that declining state for some time during which a vivid memory flashed into my mind. Years before, I'd once discovered Rachel's parents' cat with an injured mouse in its mouth. I'd crouched down, balancing on the balls of my feet, pulled the mouse free of the cat's jaws and placed it gently on the floor. It had dragged itself into the shelter of my raised feet and just sat there, shocked and terrified, unable to do anything else. The image described exactly what I was feeling at that moment in the prayer room.

I heaved my head up from its place between my knees and cranked my aching eyes across at Pete. He was still staring at me. I wondered if he could sense what was happening to me or if he was simply lost in thought.

I summoned up all my energy and shoved a quiet request for help out of my mouth and into the room. It was like trying to lift a dead weight from the floor up to a shoulder-high surface.

A moment later Pete was kneeling beside me. He motioned for Paul to join us. I simply sat, like the injured mouse, unable to do anything to help myself. I closed my eyes and sensed that Pete and

Paul were both praying even though there were no audible sounds.

The atmosphere grew thick with God's presence. My spine tingled and a rushing sensation inside my head swept from the base of my neck over the top of my skull to my eyes. I felt my arms being lifted, stretched out in front of me and held there. Pete and Paul had one each, and Pete began to pray in an audible whisper that God would restore me.

Calmness seeped into my mind and body like water trickling gently down a rivulet. Gradually the weight lifted from my heart and my soul and my body. I felt as if I had been parched with thirst and was now gulping down litres of cool water.

Pete began to talk about Moses and the way in which once, when the Israelites were fighting an important battle, if Moses held his arms up things went well, but if he let his arms drop the Israelites started losing. When Moses became too tired to hold his arms up, two men supported them and winning the battle became a team effort. I smiled inwardly to myself at the thought of being compared to Moses but realised that in a very real way, the team and I were engaged in a battle, albeit a spiritual one in which the "fighting" was being done through our persistent, courageous prayers.

To my enormous relief, the bleak emptiness was lifting and my strength and energy were returning. Paul and Pete's prayers kept coming and then, eventually, they slowed into silence.

I was still tired but I climbed to my feet, thanking Pete and Paul for their prayers and allowing a large grin to fill my face. I shook my head and my legs to revive them and felt humble and grateful. I'd never been too comfortable about being vulnerable in front of others but that evening I'd had no choice. I wasn't sure what had happened to me or why, but Pete and Paul had come to my assistance and in the process demonstrated the love, compassion and patience that is supposed to define a Christian community.

In the immediate aftermath of the bizarre and unpleasant experience, I wondered if it had been the pressure of leading the team that had got on top of me. I supposed it was possible that my experience had been a result of not having had enough sleep for a couple of nights. It even crossed my mind that it might have been some kind of spiritual assault. Whatever it had been, I was thankful that it'd passed. I could try to forget about it and concentrate on leading the team.

Swiss Phil

The afternoon following my physical, mental and spiritual nosedive and subsequent recovery, my team and I began to get stuck into some social action.

The United Reformed church on Newquay's high street hosted a daily soup kitchen for homeless people in the town. We had agreed that a couple of team members would go along each day to help out. Matt and Tim headed off to get stuck in. We couldn't have known at the time but it would turn out to be an unexpectedly fortuitous partnership.

The rest of the team headed down to Fistral beach, prepared for an afternoon of manual labour. There was a large half-pipe for skateboarders that needed to be dismantled. I'd volunteered the team's assistance and the ramp's owner had gratefully accepted.

Dismantling the ramp took hours and was heavy, oily work. At one point I was helping to lower a towering section of ramp only to have a stream of stagnant, stinking water that had gathered in a pipe pour over my head.

We hadn't been working for long when I noticed

that Paul Chowdry was deep in conversation with the owner of the ramp, a Swiss engineer called Phil. Knowing Paul's track record, I wondered how long the conversation would last.

Half an hour later they were still going, both men seemingly welded to the flat centre section of the ramp, their arms swinging with expressive gestures. We hauled sections of ramp around their discussion, puffing, sweating and grunting with exertion.

As the team and I dragged and stacked, I prayed silently for wisdom for Paul and openness for Phil.

An hour passed and although Paul and Phil had been forced to move, the conversation continued. I overheard a snippet in which Paul was explaining, with conviction, that it was often pride that kept us from admitting our need for God. I was amazed. Paul and Phil had only just met but Paul was saying things that cut right to the heart of the matter and Phil appeared to be taking it quite well!

Eventually the ramp was dismantled and stacked and Paul and Phil were shaking hands. The team and I hadn't volunteered to help with the aim of slipping in a sneaky preach, but the fact that while we'd helped God had taken the opportunity to make sure that Phil heard the gospel from Paul was a top-quality bonus.

When we got back to the hall, I ducked into the prayer room, wrote Phil's name with a fat marker-pen on a sheet of paper and stuck it among the scores of others that clung to the walls. The room looked as if a hyperactive child had tried to wallpaper it.

As I ran my eyes over the names, Liam's made me stop. I felt a jab of excitement. Thinking about our odd meeting made me smile. I was almost certain that we hadn't seen the last of him that week. I couldn't have known how soon the feeling would turn into reality.

Eye Stabber

On the beach that night, I found myself in imminent danger.

I was sitting on the sand with Matt and Angela. The three of us were facing in the direction of the sea and chatting when a commotion behind us made us look round. A broad, bulky man dressed in several layers of dirty clothing and wearing a knitted balaclava was screaming aggressively at a group of teenagers. Terrified, they scattered like bowling pins and the man lurched on – towards us.

A moment later he was towering over us, his bulging eyes weighing us up from puffy sockets in the top of his red face. He held his arm out at full stretch to steady himself. In his hand he clutched a cider bottle. It didn't require an expert to realise that he was not only drunk but also mentally ill and seriously angry.

"D'jew know ooh smacked my bruver?" He poked his face at each of us in turn. Alcoholic fumes swamped us like a cloud of gas.

I guessed he could be referring to an incident that Matt, Angela and I had witnessed on our way down to the beach earlier that evening – a guy had been smashed over the head with a bottle. Matt had recognised the victim from the soup kitchen, where he'd helped earlier that day. Before we could help though, the guy had staggered away with blood from the wound streaming down his face.

"Wen I find the bloke that dun my bruver in, I'm gonna stab his eyes out!" spat the man standing over us.

The three of us assured him that we didn't know anything about who had attacked his brother. Angela mentioned the help we had tried to give. The man didn't seem to hear her. He was too busy staring at me. I'd caught his eye and held it for a millisecond too long. I was about to regret it.

"You want some f****** trouble?" He jabbed the bottle at me. My pulse rate leapt. I pulled my head back in surprise and closed my fingers around the damp sand behind me.

"No, not at all." I wasn't lying. I really didn't want my eyes stabbed out or anything even close to it.

"Cause if you fink I'm jokin, I'll kick your f****** edd in." Flecks of saliva flicked out at me and he raised his cider bottle so that it was level with his shoulder and looked scarily like a club.

I didn't think he was joking at all. The man was winding himself up and I didn't rate my chances of reasoning with him. I fired muddled emergency prayers at God like flares from a stricken ship.

As I was weighing up the odds of spending the night in hospital against making it back to my sleeping bag, Matt, who was sitting less than half a metre to my left, pulled out a sneaky get-out-of-jail-free card.

"It's OK Sonny," he said (far too calmly, given the circumstances). I turned to look at him in surprise. How had Matt known the man's name? "Sonny" seemed as shocked as me. The pair of us looked at Matt.

"You came into the soup kitchen today," Matt reminded "Sonny".

Sonny's expression clouded over as if he was dragging his memories out of a dusty cupboard deep inside his confused head. And then, after what seemed like far too long, recognition!

"Yeah! I remember you. . ." For a moment a flicker of recollection appeared in his eyes. His head seemed to jolt forward a fraction and the edges of his cracked lips turned up slightly. As quickly as it'd come though, the expression disappeared, as if a blanket had been thrown over it and, without another word, Sonny turned and lumbered away.

Relief washed over me like a bucket of cold water. I exhaled deeply, feeling unbelievably grateful that Matt had agreed to help out at the soup kitchen. My relief was quickly interrupted though by an overwhelming sense that although Sonny was a fellow human being who needed a mountain of love, care and help, I had absolutely no idea whatsoever how I might offer any of those things to him.

He was clearly a walking tragedy and I was supposed to know a God who could help people like him. But the problem seemed huge. I couldn't imagine where God would start. Jesus would have known what to say to Sonny and he'd have known just how to say it. But I wasn't Jesus and I didn't have a clue what to do. I was just glad to have my face intact. I wondered what kind of Christian that made me – or what kind of team leader for that matter. . .

Sand People

On Wednesday evening the sun was hidden behind thick clouds and a damp mist harassed the holiday town.

No one on the team, including me, felt like doing much except drinking hot chocolate. Cosying-up was not an option, however, so Pete, Sophie, the two Paul's and I decided to shake off our lethargy with a walk. We quickly found ourselves on an alleyway known as the "tram tracks" that ran along the top of the cliffs at the edge of town.

The view across the beach and out to sea was inspiring in spite of the weather. We stared down at the grey, tide-washed sand. Two people, who looked the size of ants, were walking their bounding dog along the edge of the water. Someone had scrawled large letters in the sand. I couldn't work out what they were meant to say but their presence prompted an idea to drop into my mind. As I turned to the others to announce it, it became obvious that Sophie and the two Pauls had had the same thought.

"I reckon we should get down there and write something massive in the sand!" I blurted, wanting to get the suggestion out before they had a chance to do likewise. They all laughed.

"I was going to say the same thing." Paul hauled his drum further up onto his shoulder.

Pete didn't look convinced and explained that he wasn't sure what good it would do. I wasn't sure either but as the thought had occurred to several of us at once, and as writing something in the sand wouldn't take all night, it seemed like we might as well do it.

"It'll be worship – we'll write something, pray as we go, Paul can drum and we'll offer the whole thing to God." I threw the suggestion into the air as the five of us headed for the slip road.

It would only be a small, simple thing but it would be fun and we'd be doing it for God.

As we hurried down the steep, winding road that dropped to the sand behind the massive Springbok nightclub, we chatted excitedly about what to write. Several suggestions were thrown around but most were too long. If the letters were going to be large we didn't want to be writing out an entire chapter from the Bible. We needed something simple and easy to spell.

In the end we decided on JESUS IS LORD in full capitals. It was short and to the point and it would be good to announce it in the sand on which so many people partied each night.

Sophie, Paul Chowdry and I began scrawling the words as the daylight faded. Pete and drummer-Paul perched on a near-by rock and Paul beat out a pulsing rhythm. A light, misty rain, blown in from the sea, whispered across the beach as we worked.

The thump of the drum echoed and rumbled across the wet sand and climbed confidently up the rutted surface of the towering black cliffs. Paul, Sophie and I were spread far out from each other, shuffling along, gouging out mini-trenches in the sand with coarse stones the size of boxers' fists. As huge letters began to emerge beneath my feet, I broke into a fierce sweat.

High above us on the cliff, people began to gather and look down, their attention captured by the rhythm of the drum dipping and rising and by the almost frantic activity of three sand-authors. I prayed silently, offering my body, my soul, my efforts, the beach and the people watching to God. I was worshipping my creator with my whole body and with my creativity. Everything I was doing and being was aimed at him; my move-ments, my sweating, the making of marks in the earth – the stuff which my body was made of and to which, one day, it would return. My worship was raw and heartfelt and all-encompassing and, since worshipping God was what I was made for, my soul and my heart were at peace in the midst of all the activity.

And then it was finished; massive letters, hewn out of the sand, proclaiming like an advertisement that the God-man, Jesus, was Lord.

Paul, Sophie and I, panting from our exertion, joined Paul and Pete on the rock. Paul continued to drum and the five of us prayed out loud for New-quay and everyone who found themselves in the town that night, and I felt alive and full of hope – as if something significant was about to happen.

Among other things, and unbeknown to us, God would be using our prayers to prepare someone we'd already met for another encounter with him.

American Beauty

Sophie burst through the prayer room doorway, allowing light from the main hall to spill across the red carpet and flood the scattered paper, pens, candles, mugs and other debris with a flat glare.

"I've just spent the last two hours talking to Liam about Jesus!" She was out of breath and I guessed she'd run from somewhere to share the news.

"*American* Liam?" I'd thought it would be me that would come across him again, so I was surprised to hear it'd been Sophie.

"Yes!" Sophie stepped into the room, allowing the door to swing closed. A calm ambience returned as the glare from the hall lights was shut out. Pete and Suzie, who were in the prayer room with me, sat up attentively and tuned in.

"*Where*? And how come?" I stood up and dragged a chair over to Sophie so that she could sit down. Perching on the edge of it, she explained that a few hours after we'd returned from gouging huge words into the sand, she and Angela had gone to On the Rocks bar and spotted Liam. They'd recognised him from the car park conversation I'd had with him during our first night in town and introduced themselves.

Apparently still a little weirded-out from his God-encounter with me earlier in the week, Liam had been doubly shocked to find someone who knew his name, in a bar that it transpired he'd never been to before and where he had gone to meet a guy he hardly ever spent time with. He'd soon recovered however, and spent the rest of the evening with the girls asking searching questions and discussing the possibility that God wanted to get his attention. When they'd parted company, Liam told Sophie that he was interested in going along to a local church.

It was such a neat follow-on to the episode that had begun on our first night in town that I had to give a spontaneous burst of applause to express my excitement. Pete gave a satisfied nod and offered to go and make everyone a cup of tea by way of a mini-celebration.

I felt plumped up with fresh motivation because being involved in a story like Liam's was downright brilliant and fulfilling. I knew it was likely that my team and I would witness only a tiny apparent response to our prayers and conversations that week because God's work is often the kind that goes on unseen in people's hearts and anything we said or did would be a single link in a long chain of events. Because this was the way things often were, the un-manufactured, genuine neatness of the two God-filled encounters with Liam were a special mission-bonus and reminded me of the value and worth of the mission team being in Newquay to pray and live out our faith.

Fantastic Family Picnic

I'd been missing Rachel and Hannah all week, so on Thursday afternoon, while things in Newquay were relatively quiet, I drove to Falmouth to find them.

As I pulled into the drive of the place they were staying, a heart-warming scene greeted me. Rachel was sitting on a low wall in the shade of a leafy tree. Hannah was standing patiently between her mum's knees, dressed in a funky pair of dungarees and clutching her favourite teddy-bear. The sight of the two of them made my heart leap and tears crept into the corners of my eyes. Hannah looked so much bigger than I'd remembered! It'd only been a few days since I'd last seen her but, by the look of things, she'd been doing a whole lot of growing.

I leapt out of my car, gathered the pair of them into my arms and squeezed them tightly in a huge hug. Their familiar shapes and smells filled my body with a delightful calmness. I hadn't realised quite how much I'd been missing them. In those first few seconds I already knew how difficult it would be to leave them later that afternoon and return to my team.

After a gorgeous lunch of sausage sandwiches, washed down with cups of tea, Rachel and I sat on the balcony of the flat and talked about how the mission was going.

As I told some of the stories that the week had thrown up, Hannah toddled happily back and forth, bringing us her toys and books and entertaining us with her antics.

I told Rachel how well the team had gelled together and how our prayers and efforts had gathered momentum and how praying until the early hours of each morning had become our habit. She laughed in surprise at the idea of me praying until the early hours – probably because she knew how much I loved to sleep! I guessed she was also a little concerned in case I wanted us to continue the habit once we'd returned home to London. . .

We poured more tea and sliced up some cake and I gabbled on, telling Rachel that no one on the team was bored, or wanted to go home as I'd worried at the start, and that none of them seemed to think I'd been foolish or hasty in organising the mission. In fact, I told her, the team seemed to think the opposite – that the mission had been a great idea and that a mountain of things had already been achieved in the lives of people that we'd met.

Rachel was particularly impressed when I got

around to telling her that the team had even got organised enough to have a shopping, cooking and cleaning rota that really worked!

I told Rachel how tough it had been to be separated from her and Hannah for the week. In fact, it had been a big sacrifice for all three of us. Rachel had been finding it a struggle, although Hannah loved it because her doting grandparents were at the flat in Falmouth and she was the entire focus of their attentions.

Before I left, Rachel and I held each other for a long time. I wanted to be able to remember what she felt like when I was climbing into my sleeping bag in the basement back in Newquay at five in the morning. I could feel the sour wrench of separation in my belly as I climbed into my car.

I rolled down the window and Rachel held Hannah up for me to kiss. As she put her back down beside her, Rachel said something that would be a huge encouragement to me for the remaining days of the mission and for many months afterwards.

She reminded me that the work that the team and I were doing through our prayers and our frank conversations about God was eternal and foundational. Eternal, because it consisted of inviting people into a relationship with God that starts now and goes on for ever. Foundational because in years to come others would build on what we'd prayed and said and done, just as we were already building on the prayers, words and actions of many before us.

Driving away from Falmouth was horrible but Rachel's profound words of encouragement were rolling around inside my head and wrapping themselves around my heart. They gave me fresh anticipation and enthusiasm for getting stuck into whatever lay ahead in the three days of the mission that remained.

Mass Confusion

On Friday night the team and I got to the beach early and prayed together on the sand. Feeling excited about what the night would bring, we lit our flaming torches, piled up bottles of water to give away and began to strike up conversations with the people on the sand around us.

Clubbers came and went and gratefully took the water and showered us with genuine questions about God and Jesus, life and death, sex and drugs and not knowing what to think or believe.

The first time I looked at my watch, it was after 4am. I could almost hear my air mattress and sleeping bag calling to me from the hall. My eyes ached and I needed to sleep.

Sleep was going to have to wait though. A skinny, thoughtful-looking young man sporting a Bob-Dylan-in-the-sixties look appeared from my blind spot and crouched down, perching on the balls of his feet beside me. He was fidgeting like a nervous mouse.

Without warning he began talking about Christianity. Or rather, he began giving me his unsolicited views on Christianity. I could only assume he'd spoken to another member of my team earlier in the evening and either thought it'd been me or didn't care and just wanted to have a religious-themed chat.

I listened while "Dylan" (he hadn't told me his *actual* name) filled me in on the fact that he'd given Christianity some consideration but had eventually dismissed it as unsuitable as he felt it was too institutional. Buddhism, he explained, was more in line with his way of thinking about things. As he spoke he regularly pushed sections of his thick hair randomly back and forth across his forehead.

As returning to my sleeping bag was temporarily off the agenda, I decided to take the opportunity to introduce Dylan to Jesus. While he'd been speaking, it had occurred to me that in his search for meaning, he might have confused *doing* Christianity the religion with *knowing* Jesus Christ the person. I put this possibility to him.

He replied with a line I'd heard scores of times on the beach; that Jesus was simply a good, wise fellow whose life and teachings had got blown out of all proportion and ended up being used by corrupt leaders who abused their power for their own ends.

Fortunately, I'd given this hypothesis a fair bit of thought and study.

I tried to rub the tiredness out of my eyes and face with sandy fingers and put it to Dylan that the gospels in which Jesus' words were recorded are considered authentic historical documents. In other words, I told him, we could be pretty certain that Jesus actually said the things it is claimed he said.

Dylan had no problem with that. He'd studied the gospels at school – which was good as it meant that we had a foundation to build the rest of my point on.

It therefore followed, I continued, that we could take the things Jesus said with some seriousness.

Once again, Dylan appeared content to accept my logic.

There were little grains of sand under my

tongue that I'd accidentally pushed into my mouth when I'd attempted to rub the tiredness away. I explained to Dylan (while trying to extricate the sand with my forefinger) that having read the gospels on many occasions, I could say confidently that the writers leave us in no doubt that Jesus believed himself to be *The* Son of God. "It's not possible to misunderstand Jesus' words as recorded in the gospels." I went on, "*Jesus* didn't think of himself as *just a good bloke*."

Dylan ran a considered finger over his pointed chin, computing what I'd said. I picked at my tongue, removing grains of sand and wiping them on my leg.

"Really, we're only left with three options."

Dylan turned his head towards me for a moment before returning it to its former position, facing towards the sea.

"Either Jesus was a nutter. . ." I thought of Sonny threatening to stab my eyes out as I said this.

"No one thinks Jesus was a nutter," Dylan interrupted, shaking his head from side to side in rapid movements.

"If he wasn't a nutter, he could have been a liar. . ."

Dylan's brow furrowed and he looked down at the sand for a moment.

"But if he lied about being the Son of God, then he wouldn't be a *good* teacher – and anyway, insisting on being God's son got him crucified! Surely, if he'd been lying he would have come clean long before the Romans slaughtered him?"

The edge of Dylan's mouth cracked in a slight smile. He'd clearly guessed what I was going to say next.

"So if he wasn't mad or a liar, we're left with the possibility that he was telling the truth, and if he *was*, then his words are without doubt, the most important ever spoken."

Dylan's mouth broke into a full smile and he raised his hands above his head and shook them.

"You've got a good argument!" he laughed. "I have to say, I've not thought about it like that. I'll need to think this through. . ."

I rocked back on my bottom, staring out towards the sea and feeling pleased that Dylan had the integrity to say he'd give his current ideas some further thought. I realised that I still didn't know Dylan's real name. I wasn't about to find out either. Before I could ask him he uncurled himself from his crouching position and stood up, interrupting the possibility of having an imminent spiritual rethink by announcing:

"I want you to meet one of my friends – he'll be interested to speak to you."

I suppressed a yawn and looked up at him. I wanted to go to bed.

He swept his thin arm in an arc, motioning at the people on the beach around us. What he said as he did it punctured my mind and lit it up like a firework.

"Everyone's so confused."

It was as if Dylan had just snapped a profound and incredible word-photograph. He'd seen to the heart of what was going on around us and grasped the truth of it all and he'd announced it, blasé, in the middle of the party.

In three words, Dylan had summed up our generation.

There was no time to pick him up on the thought – he'd disappeared off along the sand to fetch the friend he wanted me to meet.

Jesus Wept

Richard was high on ecstasy and stumbled frequently as Dylan led him towards me. It looked as if Dylan was dragging an injured comrade out of a combat zone. As I watched them making their way over the sand, I groaned inwardly. I was exhausted and not in the mood for making conversation with someone who was off his face on drugs.

Having delivered his friend onto the sand beside me and told me the guy's name, Dylan wandered off again and disappeared from my view. I wasn't sure what he'd been expecting me to say to Richard but I supposed anything along the same lines as the things he and I had spoken about earlier.

I looked down at Richard. He'd managed to prop himself up on his elbow and was gurning with his lower jaw and smacking his lips together. A debate about Jesus' divinity didn't strike me as something Richard would appreciate right then.

I offered him a bottle of water instead, which he took gratefully and began to sip. When he'd had time to settle himself, we started to speak. Although his words were slowed by the influence of the ecstasy, I was surprised to find that the conversation was coherent and became deep quite quickly.

Richard told me about his boarding school education and his parents' large home in Somerset and then, without warning, he dropped a bombshell.

"One afternoon in the school holidays," he was fiddling with the lid from the water bottle as he spoke, "I got home from the local shops and my brother was waiting on the drive and he told me not to go into the garden because Dad had killed himself."

I drew a deep breath through my nostrils.

"And they wouldn't let me see him. . ." Richard's words were rimmed with bleak emotion. He sniffed hard and I thought he might be crying but when I shot him a quick glance I couldn't see any tears.

I wanted to help him in some way but felt unqualified to comment on the size of the tragedy that had bulldozed his life. I guessed Dylan had told Richard that he'd spoken to me about God – perhaps Dylan had thought I could help his friend sort his head out. I didn't think there was much chance of my doing that.

Tiredness banged at the inside of my head, demanding that I pay it attention. I did my best to ignore it and prayed, asking God for the wisdom to know what to say to Richard and when to keep quiet.

Richard went on to tell me that as a child, he'd spent several holidays at his grandpa's home. They'd slept in twin beds in the same room and his grandpa had prayed before the pair of them went to sleep every night. The prayers had woven into Richard a belief that God was real but he couldn't balance that idea with the appalling reality of his dad committing suicide.

"Why would God let that happen to me?" he asked.

I stayed silent. He looked up at me, his eyes rolling towards the back of his head slightly. He might have been high but he still wanted an answer.

I didn't know what to say. I didn't know why it had happened. I believed in a God who sees more horror than any human being will ever see and yet is the source of love. I believed in a God who has the power to do anything yet allows suffering. At that moment though, these weren't things for me to say to Richard, who was stuffed with sour emptiness and who felt he needed some kind of straightforward explanation.

I took another deep breath, pulled my knees up to my chest and leant my chin on them, letting the air in my lungs escape in a slow, inaudible sigh. When I eventually spoke, it was to offer Richard something that I knew in theory but had never had to put into practice. It was the possibility that, in spite of what had happened, God wanted to mend his hurt and help him make some sense of things. It was the best I could do. Nothing really tragic had ever happened to me. My questions and struggles with God had been about different things. That didn't stop me from believing, however, that whatever tragedy anyone experienced, nothing was outside God's ability to heal completely.

Richard talked for a long time and for the most part I kept silent.

It was beginning to get light when I offered to pray for him. He seemed keen and sat up, running his tongue around the inside of his dry top lip.

I put my left hand on his shoulder and ached at God. Eventually I found some words. I prayed a gentle, steady prayer. I asked God to make himself real to Richard, to mend and help and comfort him. I meant it.

When I'd finished we stood up together and shook the sand off our trousers. The sea lapped at the sand just a few feet away from us. The tide had swollen right up the beach, washing away the scars of the night. The scene struck me as being a great picture of God's love: Unstoppable. Unfathomable. Vast.

She Who Seeks Finds. . .

In the very early hours of Sunday morning five members of the team decided to pay a final visit to the huge stone cross that stands on the hill above the town overlooking the ocean. The team's week had begun there and it seemed a good place to bring things to a close.

The canopy of the sky curved vast and endless overhead, stuffed with stars and satellites, as the five team members slowly climbed the deserted, grassy hill, away from the lights and noise of the town towards the calm darkness of the summit.

The night air was chilly. They pulled their hoodies up close to their necks and wrapped their arms around their middles to keep warm. The white, stencilled letters stamped across the backs of their tops spelling 24-7 Prayer poked out of the darkness like cat's eyes.

At the top of the hill they spread out around the cross, faced out towards the four compass points and thanked God for a brilliant week.

As soon as they'd finished praying, Paul Chowdry and Matt helped each other to clamber up onto the cross. Soon the other three followed. They laughed and pulled and shoved and eventually all five were clinging to parts of the cross like passengers covering a train in India.

As they dangled there together in the darkness, footsteps and a voice broke into their reverie.

"How'd you get up there?" asked a young woman who had appeared out of the darkness and stumbled up to the foot of the cross. "And anyone got any rizzla?" She thrust a hand up at the cross and twiddled her thumb against her fingers in an action that resembled rolling a cigarette. A stack of bangles on her wrist clattered together with a tinny-sounding clink.

"No rizzla, sorry!" Paul Chowdry sounded genuinely apologetic.

The young woman tipped her head back and tried to focus on the people dangling like bizarre fruit from the enormous cross.

"So, how'd you get up?" Her tone suggested she wanted to join them.

"Give us your hands." Angela stretched an arm down towards the woman, opening and closing her fist in a grasping action as she did so. Chris and Paul offered their arms too, taking care not to topple off the cross in the process.

The young woman reached up, pressing her body against the rough stone of the cross, and clutched at the wiggling fingers being offered to her. The various sets of fingers closed around each other and there was leg-scrambling and elbow-grabbing, grunts of exertion, bursts of laughter, a shout of "Careful!" and then the young woman was up, squeezed into a tiny space beside Angela, and everyone knew that everyone else was smiling even though they could barely see each other. There was more laughter and the five mission team members and a young woman whom none of them knew clung on to the great stone cross, in the dark, at 2 am on a Sunday morning in August and began to talk about what on earth they were doing there.

Survivor books...
receive as you read

Red Moon Rising
by Pete Greig

24-7 is at the centre of a prayer revival across the globe and this book gives a fantastic insight into what God is doing with ordinary prayer warriors. Read inspiring stories of people finding a new depth of heartfelt prayer and radical compassion.

double sided book

The Vision & The Vow
by Pete Greig

Has your faith become a chore where once it was a passion? Are you tired of the self-serving mentality of our culture? Join Pete Greig on the adventure of a lifetime; unlocking God's ultimate vision for your life and your community.

Diary of a Dangerous Vision
by Andy Hawthorne

This is the story of one man's dramatic conversion and the blossoming of an ever-growing group of Christians set to take Christ into the most challenging and tough urban areas.

The Truth will Set You Free
by Beth Redman

With insight and humour, Beth helps young women to find God's answers to the big questions and struggles in their lives. Thousands of teenage girls have come to trust Beth Redman's powerful and relevant teaching through her packed seminars at Soul Survivor.

Rad Lad Livin
by Mark Bowness

The perfect manual to help any lad move forward in God, tackling issues ranging from lust to identity, from brotherhood to homosexuality - this book is practical in its nature and real in its content.

survivor